FREE 'D !!!

FREE 'D !!!

A Recovery Plan

T Rose

Tiffy Rose LLC - Publishing
Jensen Beach

FREE 'D !!!   A Recovery Plan

T. Rose – Author

Harry B Gardner – Editor

Copyright © 2019 by Tiffy Rose, LLC

Cover copyright © 2019 by Tiffy Rose, LLC

All rights reserved

Including the right of reproduction

In whole or in any part in any form

While the public record of events and personal interviews

are as accurate as memories and transcription allow

– though condensed and edited –

names and precise locale data have been changed to honor privacy.

Tiffy Rose LLC – Publishing

Jensen Beach, FL

Owner – T. Rose

CEO – Harry B Gardner

http://www.tiffyrose1recovery.com

Paperback ISNB: # 978-1-7320331-2-2

E-Book ISNB: # 978-1-7320331-3-9

LCCN # 2019901641

Dedication

FREE 'D... began as my journey alone but became a caravan of many required to reach the final destination with the publication of this book. The unknown challenges and struggles ahead were not visible when I began free writing an outline and scheduled a firm release date of a completed manuscript. What I foresaw as a sunny day brisk walk on level ground ultimately required skills, discipline, and stamina by a few hardy souls to scale a jagged mountainside in the cold of winter so I could plant my victory flag on the snowy peak. My deepest gratitude to each of you for giving so generously of yourselves sheltering me from harsh winds of criticism, and tirelessly pulling the rope along, and pushing me up those last few footsteps so I could reach out to touch the mighty hand of God.

To Harry, I owe not gratitude but acceptance of his perception that good guys sometimes wear black hats and their true purpose is to challenge me to grow beyond my comfort zone. To Gideon whose courage is as great as his namesake's, for proving once again the outcome of a battle *is never certain or ordained but rests with the will of the warrior to prevail with the Lord's blessing.*

To each and every one of you who walked with me into and out of "The Big Trap: Just One Last High", you made FREE 'D our story and I am blessed by your willingness to illuminate your path through the darkness and into the light that all of us are made stronger. I hope you will see your role in making the world more aware of our plight and that our unique journey through recovery is long and lonely and without their willing hand to help we don't always make it.

To my many readers around the world, I dedicate this common journey to you with hopes you find understanding and encouragement and continue sharing with others in need your insights and wisdom to prevail against addiction.

God Bless- Rose

Contents

Foreward
xi

Introduction
1

Chapter 1.
Fear and Anger
11

Chapter 2.
Trust and Hope
21

Chapter 3.
One of the Good Guys!
38

Chapter 4.
Stepping Stones and the Fight!
61

Chapter 5.
The Therapists Couch
79

Chapter 6.
Family Affair
98

Chapter 7.
Transcendental Meditation
132

Chapter 8.
A Smokey Room Brawl
152

Chapter 9.
Other Pitfalls in the Rooms
174

Chapter 10.
Spirituality
194

Chapter 11.
A Rising Star...
210

Chapter 12.
My Sanctuary
225

Foreward

Tiffany Rose Baker was an accomplished young career woman on a fast track ascent up the ladder in the new age of technology when the scourge of cocaine shattered her dream of making it to the top to break the glass ceiling. We followed her down in the free fall from the spotlight of success through the glittering clubs and nightlife walking the mean streets and dark alleys of addiction in "The Big Trap- Just One Last High." Follow her now as she crawls from the trap battered and broken defying the demon to drag her back into the darkness searching for redemption and recovery into a new life. Share her journey with a few trusted sponsors and hear the dark truths unveiled on therapists' couches as she walks twelve steps through a hundred smoky rooms shaping a new dream she could believe in.

The long road back.... is now my freedom.

Introduction

This was the final betrayal.

I didn't want to believe it when Jared asked for my wedding ring. I stood staring at him in disbelief, confusion, and dismay filling my mind realizing maybe I didn't really know the man standing before me after all. Yes, he looked like Jared; 5'10", curly sun-bleached hair on his head, a lean taut well-muscled physique, skin golden brown from years in the south Florida sun digging ditches and laying untold miles of sprinkler pipe in the ground. But would the man I happily married and called my husband in good times and bad, hoping still today we would renew our failing relationship and our marriage, be standing in front of me demanding the ring that sealed our union be given back? Was this really the man I married? Was this the end of all we struggled for seemingly being mugged by a stranger demanding my ring or my life?

Bewilderment showing in my face I asked, "What did you say?"

"Give me your ring, I want to go pawn it and get some more coke, I've got to work today and I need a boost before I go." He replied.

I couldn't fathom what he was saying; he wanted to sell my wedding ring for drugs, the only real thing we had managed to hold on to through all this craziness. The ring, at least for me, was a symbol of my love and commitment to the marital promise that I faithfully honored that bonded us and held us together. Wearing it was my constant reminder for where there was a will there was a way together to prevail against all the things pushing against us and taking us down an even darker path. It was my strength when I was at my lowest with Jared and the ring was like a cross I unconsciously touched and turned when ugly temptations welled up inside to avenge his rejection of me or my own faithfulness to my wedding vows before him and God. It was everything it was supposed to be for a woman committed to doing her part in a partnership of marriage for better or worse. Now he wants it and all it stands for to pawn or sell for a tiny amount of cocaine.

Oh my God. No, this can't be happening this isn't real, was all I could think. He grabbed my hand, pulled the ring off my finger, turned away, and headed out the door stating flatly without any emotion I could discern, "I'll be back in half an hour with more dope." For long and surreal minutes maybe even an hour after Jared pulled the door closed behind him and I heard the sound of his big diesel pick-up truck fade away in the distance, I stood motionless leaning on the kitchen counter tears flowing hard and steady barely able to breathe feeling dazed and numb. The lump in my dry throat had grown slowly larger and I believed I would slowly suffocate with my mind stuck on a single question repeating itself soundlessly over and over again. "How did it all come to this?"

In slow-motion procession days and nights of highs and lows paraded through my mind filling in the spaces that were the years Jared and I were together. I watched close up and from far away as quiet acts of love and kindness in candlelight reminded me why I loved him and that love I had given him was real enough and strong enough for him in the early years. The elusive light of love floating through my mind alternated with loud dark bouts of cocaine-fueled anger and rage filling rooms in our home and glaring stares in public places we had been together. I heard and felt the warm and romantically cherished 'I love you' and the ugly stabbing pain of 'you selfish bitch' streaming in and out repeating like a chorus of a song stuck in your mind.

The fierce pain in my hands from clutching tightly the edge of the countertop brought me back to the reality of Jared's departure. The waves of nausea had receded and no more tears could flow from my burning eyes. I felt dizzy, unsteady, and couldn't breathe through my stuffed nose and my throat was parched. I took a hesitant first step and shuffled a few more slowly and sat down at the kitchen table putting my head down on my crossed arms hoping the spinning feeling would pass and I wouldn't pass out. I felt truly empty and alone but it was not a new and unknown feeling owing to Jared's devastating admission a year ago he was unfaithful and cheated on me with other women.

As the day became night sitting at the kitchen table and it became clear that Jared was most likely high and half-drunk with another woman in some bar somewhere, I accepted what started as a happy dream with my shining knight had become the ultimate nightmare. My love had gone out the door with my ring that he would so casually give away... never to be returned.

The beautiful new house we bought together by saving every penny we could and living thrifty was now in foreclosure. The irrigation business we started together with a single employee and me working with them after getting off at my day job and on Saturdays was crumbling. Our reputation for good work and dependability that earned us a constant stream of new customers and bigger jobs that we steadily hired and trained new employees and bought equipment to do was slowly destroyed because a couple of drinks after twelve and fourteen-hour days and casual Sunday drug use became heavy addiction with Jared erratic and more unpredictable each day. I had quit my job in the late stages of pregnancy and stayed home after Crystal's birth, but after seven months of being the good mother and dutiful wife, I was in no shape to work effectively because I too had become addicted to cocaine.

The answer to the question still lingering in my mind as the clock approached midnight, 'How did all this happen?' had a very simple answer, a truth that we had constantly denied was happening to both of us. Denial could be so easy and it was all the way down to this bottom. In a cold moment of clarity I saw and accepted the bitter truth at the kitchen table in the wee hours of the morning with the mortgage payments long overdue and no food in the house, drugs had ruined my picture-perfect life. Sadly true also was the toll cocaine had taken on me physically and mentally that was clearly visible in the harsh light of reality. Escalating from casual Sunday use in the beginning to sharing an 8-ball of cocaine a night week in and week out I was underweight, mentally ragged, and recently had become mostly uncaring about my personal appearance. The devotional road of long hours and self-sacrifice that empowered our shared dream of personal and business success and made it a reality, had steadily given way to being stealthy functional addicts on a steep slope down to the poorhouse leaving both of us but shadows of the successes we were.

Sunlight streaming through the window woke me the following morning still sitting at the kitchen table. The rationally minded realist I had been for a short time in the darkness, mentally examining the shared consequences of alcohol, drugs, and infidelity and the reasons Jared and I could and would quit immediately... disappeared quickly in the harsh morning light. Stiff, sore, and emotionally drained with a realization I was experiencing the first stage of withdrawal, my steadfast commitment to saving us and our business from total destruction defaulted. The desperation of the immediate reality, I only wanted to get high quickly to ease the pain filling my world.

Jared finally returned home the following evening looking haggard and strung out from coke, alcohol, and lack of sleep. He came through the door with the kicked dog look I had seen before when he screwed up badly and wanted me to feel sorry for him instead of being angry and mad. He looked me straight in the eyes with feigned sadness and self-reproach to begin pleading his case for understanding and forgiveness.

"I am so, so sorry Tiffany. I got messed up trying to score the coke and I was just going to have a drink or two while I was waiting for my connection to show up. I really don't know what happened but I woke up in my truck with no coke and no money, but I had to go to work you know. I really am sorry I let this happen. I will make it up to you, I promise, I really will get some more coke for us and get your ring back as soon as I get paid from the job I am doing now," he stated gravely.

All I could do was stand there in the entryway and listen to his woeful tale knowing full well most of it was a lie if not all of it. We both knew I was in bad need of a couple of lines and he knew there was little if anything I could do to help myself and not be completely at his mercy at this point. He knew the obvious facts looking at me standing there sad and disappointed because he had left me alone, hungry, and broke, while he was off playing his games. I was fearful, disheveled, hungry, and overwhelmed by the desperation of our situation and what we were going to do. I had paced the house and the yard all day alternately crying and pleading, begging and demanding, threatening and promising, engaging in verbal confrontations with Jared's imagined presence. I was completely vulnerable to him and his choices and with a baby to feed and care for I was totally dependent on him as well. I no longer had a job or income of my own and no longer had my own car, because it had been sold three months previous to pay the long overdue utility bills and put food on the table.

"Tomorrow honey, for sure I will get us a big bag and we can hit the grocery store too and we will be okay again," he said as he walked to the bedroom, fell onto the bed fully dressed, leaving me standing there feeling numb and lifeless. It went even further downhill than I thought it could ever go, much farther because for every step up we would take toward things getting better we took two or even three or four steps back down toward the bottom.

The months ahead would bring plenty of moving from apartment to apartment as using was still the most important thing on our minds. Months became a couple of years and brought more horrible realities to our lives as Jared's compulsion to use, drink and have sex with anyone he could, ultimately and quickly destroyed any love I had left for him.

The final straw for any hope of there ever being again an "us" would occur the night he sent me to get money from his silent business partner to buy some drugs off the street at 3 a.m. in the morning. After a couple of hours of scurrying to get the money and meet the dealer and score, I finally arrived home just before 7 a.m. and found Crystal in the bed with Jared and she was moaning, crying, and naked. My beautiful little baby girl ran to me from across the bed her blue eyes filled with the saddest look I had ever seen, and something in me went cold and dark. I completely lost it. Pain, anger, confusion, and shame engulfed me all at the same horrible gut-wrenching moment.

I truly wanted to believe he had taken off her wet diaper to stop her crying, knowing I would re-diaper her soon enough when I came back and he passed out at some point. But for the natural protective mother in me, it was a point of no return, no more chances, and the last bit of trust and respect I had for Jared was lost and gone forever.

My fragile world of hope and happiness that I was clinging to shattered. The dream was broken, my husband was a liar and cheater, my career was gone by my own drug use, and my innocent child may have been sexually abused just as I was when I was young. The world at large was suddenly broken, all the pieces began drifting further and further apart. Something in me just couldn't believe what I saw or what I felt about the entire dilemma we had let ourselves be dragged into. Everything slowly became vague and gray, all thinking and reasoning shut down, and I felt somehow broken and doubted anything would ever be right or normal or the way it was again. The gray world steadily became very dark and almost totally silent until I found safe and secure the ominous noise and harsh light of each day could no longer penetrate into the place I had gone to. Jared took me to meet some friendly people at the Shoreline Health and Wellness Center one Saturday morning after I sat silently staring into space and refusing the coke or anything else he offered me for three days and nights. *I vaguely remember* sitting in my favorite rocking chair like I did when I was pregnant with Crystal silently rocking and humming and napping all day and night except for the necessary trips to the bathroom. WHY? Jared and those nice folks wanted to know why was I doing that non-stop. WHY? What emotional crisis had happened to me they insistently asked day and night? Tell us what happened so we can help you they pleaded. I guess perhaps it was as they said an emotional crisis I suffered because by telling them they were right about everything they were saying, as Jared begged me to do, and demanding I never, never tell them we were doing drugs for over three years were they going to let me go home and keep my baby. Actually, I didn't want to go back *there* and be with Jared. No, not at all did I believe I should be with him anywhere at all. But I could not leave or lose my precious baby daughter, and I had no way to take care of her on my own, and I had no one and nowhere else I could go to find my way back to the self-sufficient woman I had once happily been. No not at all could I take Crystal and make it on my own with her, *or so I erroneously believed then much to mine and her detriment.*

Thus the decision to be released was accepted and the effects of the antipsychotic and antidepressant meds they pumped me full of day and night seemed to help and I went home after three weeks. I could not realize then just how terribly wrong the decision to go back home with Jared would be. It certainly wasn't the one I know today I would have made with a little more counseling help and being less afraid of Jared to tell them the whole truth about him and the drugs. I could and would have avoided an unnecessary path of suffering and self-destruction borne of fear and uncertainty that I alone was unprepared and ill-informed to deal with.

As surely as there was a glimmer of hope for me and Crystal for those few weeks, I was unfortunately thrust back into a world I desperately wanted to escape from. For obvious and not so obvious reasons the hamster wheel of addiction became my fate once again.

Getting high was all there was left now!

I would blindly go forward shortly after being released from the psychiatric facility to tolerate more of Jared's debauchery until finally I broke from true sanity and fled in a coke-fueled delusion to endure ten hard years on the streets. I faced a near-endless series of terrifying events, many jail incarcerations, forced rehabs, and hours that often turned into weeks high before I slept. The drug overdoses and three death experiences that only the dedicated EMTs who saved me with their quick care could believe... and the Lord who placed them there at the fatal moments to revive me each time... again, are testaments to the power of my prayers and a forgiving, loving, God and His faithful. For reasons and insights, I have already revealed herein and in my first book; The Big Trap... Just One Last High, and a few I am just now after many years of recovery and sobriety beginning to connect with and share with you, I traveled a destructive life path that no one who tried could alter. But one final day of destruction came and I did find recovery, and this is how my new life unfolded by the grace of God and all the Angels he would place in my path to get me here.

This is my story of recovery from that place of deep and great loneliness and despair. I started and completed a 12-week Christian Life Skills recovery program while incarcerated in the county jail, and I was truly ready to do whatever was necessary to find recovery and start over. Believing I had nowhere to go and no way to get there from where I was, namely in jail, I called the one person who might just care about my well-being enough to answer the phone if I called him. I dialed his number with fear and apprehension and asked him if he would pick me up from jail because I never wanted to return to the streets on which I had been living my life. By the grace of God and human compassion he told me he would and came to get me soon thereafter.

1

Fear and Anger

Lord
Enlighten what's dark in me
Strengthen what's weak in me
Mend what's broken in me
Bind what's bruised in me
Heal what's sick in me
and lastly
Revive whatever peace and
love has died in me.

It was very late in the day mid-December 2002, I was sitting in a cold holding cell feeling morose and lonely accepting I would not be seeing the judge for a special hearing I had been scheduled for that day. Expecting any moment that one of the guards would be coming to return me to my regular cell back at the jail, I put my head down and began a prayer to the Lord not to forget me and how hard I had been working to get my heart and mind ready for a new start in life I was earnestly hoping to have. A single heartbeat before the word 'Amen' was fully released out-loud into the emptiness of the cell I heard the faint shuffling steps of someone coming down the short corridor leading to the courthouses holding cell. Maybe tomorrow it will happen I said silently as I fought back the tears I knew would be coming soon. I stood up slowly feeling the stiffness of my body and my sore backside from the daylong vigil alternately sitting on the hard bench seat and pacing the few little steps I could in the tiny space that held me. I would be compliantly ready and waiting for the jailer to take me back through the tunnel that led from the main courthouse building to the alcove where the buses parked for their arrival and departure of inmates coming for their court appearances.

A short heavyset woman appeared, fiftyish with close-cropped gray hair and green eyes that matched the green of her heavily starched sheriff's uniform. The small gold black lettered name tag positioned above the left breast pocket of her uniform identified her as Whitmire. She unlocked the cell door and I was startled by her soft voice when she said apologetically, "Sorry you had to wait so long in here, but the Judge had several overlong cases on his docket before yours. He decided to stay late and hear your case anyway since you were the last scheduled hearing of the day. Follow me."

I stepped out of the cell shackled at the ankles with a chain around my waist attaching my cuffed hands in front of me at my belly. It was a harsh consequence of a criminal record that included a handgun possession charge. I headed down the corridor following closely behind trying to keep up with her brisk pace. The cold numbness in my body and my fearful anticipation of what was ahead in the courtroom caused me to stumble on the long pants leg of the jail uniform I was wearing before a dozen awkward shuffling steps had been taken.

I kept myself from a full body fall only by thrusting my cuffed hands out what little I could to keep me from slamming my face into the concrete floor. The manila file folder that contained the treasured certificates from the Rehab Program I had completed and the Petition that was the reason for my court appearance today flew from my hands and the papers tumbled out across the dirty gray floor. Officer Whitmire stopped and turned when she heard my quiet gasp of pain as my left knee and shin hit the concrete and the shackles dug into the soft flesh of my ankles. I felt that old familiar wave of nausea as the room seemed to get a little darker for a long moment. It hurt fiercely but I wasn't going to let anything delay me from seeing the judge today.

"Do you need some help?" she asked cautiously.

"No. I am fine. I'm just a little stiff and honestly, I am really nervous about this. I didn't think I was really going to see the Judge today because it had gotten so late and I figured I was going back to jail and would have to do this another day when you came for me," I said with a forced but earnest smile as I raised myself from the floor.

Standing cautiously hoping I didn't lose my balance again before the pain reaction subsided, I slowly leaned over enough to reach down and massage my knee and shin. It helped a little but I knew there was going to be some big bruises and probably swell up a bit too. I could only wish I could maybe get some ice on it before the night was over, but this was jail and that wasn't going to happen I knew.

"I will get the papers picked up and we can get moving again Officer Whitmire. I am really sorry," I said.

I took a cautious step towards the file folder and the papers that were scattered between us and was surprised when I saw her bend down quickly and with one long sweep gather everything up and hand them to me to put into the folder.

"Thank you so much. I think I am okay now. I don't want to be any later than we already are," I said genuinely appreciative of her help.

She asked if I was sure I could make it and I nodded affirmatively. She reached out her hand anyway to help assure me everything was okay before we continued on to the elevator. The door opened and we stepped in to go up three floors to the courtrooms. My heart felt like it skipped a beat or two when the doors closed and I felt the upward movement in the pit of my stomach. A big part of my future would be decided in a few minutes in a courtroom with a Judge and the States Attorney deciding my fate. I had a few moments to reflect on the path that had led me to be here with my future hanging in the balance. A lot had changed while I was in jail. Most of that change was in how I viewed my past and how the journey ahead of me was being shaped by what I had uncovered about myself and the choices I had made past and present and projected into the future I hoped was ahead of me.

 I was super thankful Judge Brown had reviewed and accepted the petition I had written and submitted to him a few weeks ago. I asked for a hearing to present my case for an early release. I was optimistic that he would grant my request given that I had been to the best of my ability a model prisoner. I had taken advantage of every opportunity to cooperate with and show respect for those working in the jail and the often thankless task they performed day in and day out with little if any respect from most inmates, male or female. I heard more than once that visitors to the jail weren't all that much better either. It took me only a few days to see and understand the vast difference in the way some of us were treated by the guards, the court people, the volunteers, or the Recovery program personnel was largely due to how we treated them. No, I didn't see any outright mistreatment even when I thought it was clearly deserved a few times.

 I had decided within a few days of being locked up I would do all I could to rehabilitate myself and signed up for the Recovery program that was offered to help me begin my long journey away from the mean streets. I completed all of the required Recovery material in the shortest amount of time possible; earning respect from the teachers and assurance from them my diligence and positive attitude would be favorably acknowledged by the judge just as it had by themselves. I had put my very best efforts into the classroom aspect of each course and engaged the teachers with an appreciation for their time and valuable insights into how to make the most of what I and the others were learning. A few of the half dozen others that I saw during various parts of the program cycle that I signed up for finished the whole program within a few days of my last day. It seemed too that the first-timers or maybe the second-timers, judging by their age and physical condition, weren't really much interested in any kind of recovery program in jail. It was a couple of souls I perceived somewhat like myself, two well-worn street girls and an older, long addicted army veteran, that saw the light at the end of a long tunnel of troubles. Older, tired, a little beat-up looking that was our common denominator. And perhaps too was a desire to try something different because what we had been doing or not doing certainly wasn't working out there for us. I wanted and needed to change my old expectations and attitude if I was going to make a positive experience of the time in jail my destructive actions had wrought. I did so and I did so with the purpose of never being isolated again without freedom for a single day living in a jail cell ever again. The Recovery program was the first big step toward that goal.

I got even more than I was expecting from some parts of the program. They were not at all what I was really expecting but perhaps it was my new attitude toward life in general and me and my choices in particular that changed my perspective. I approached the work and the discussions with our teachers the same way I had when I was in college, namely with an intention to excel. Once I got started every minute of my time had a single purpose, getting out of jail and staying clean to make a better life for myself. I am just naturally competitive and I want to be the best I can be at whatever I am doing. Even the things that got me into jail I wanted to be the best at, though clearly in hindsight that wasn't exactly a good thing then and for certain I don't ever want to be good at any of that stuff again. But just as surely as I had wanted to succeed in college for all the reasons that I did, I wanted to be the best at recovering my life in the here and now. At the moment getting out of jail early so I could get started doing that was something I truly wanted and I was in high hopes that the Judge would be wanting that too for all the reasons my petition had stated. I had a new attitude and the things that made my life the train wreck it was I wanted to forever be behind me. I was a changed woman.

Letting go of the fear was the only way I was able to achieve what I was after. The anger over so many unfair things in my life could no longer be allowed. The self-defeating rationalizations with which I had defeated myself, again and again, were no longer a part of my thinking! When I had finally let it all go, I felt a huge weight lift from my shoulders and the tired dark ugliness of the old world being erased from my thinking. With a growing belief in my own power to change my perception and my beliefs, I changed my negative attitude and behaviors into the positive outlook that I was feeling now and growing stronger every day!

I had awakened a new understanding within by the knowledge gained hour by hour, day by day, devoted to how to be a redeemed soul, all documented by the certificates earned and in my folder. The bigger question that remained, will I follow through on what I know now is the only way to have the life I hunger for again. The hard-fought successes early in my life I had earned before I had let bad judgment and unearned trust steal them from me, could all be regained and maybe even more so than before. It was up to me and those who I could truly trust to find that path to follow again. How will I implement this knowledge into my life as I work through the rubble of the past? I had a mental list of ideas and choices and a time frame that loosely formed my new life plan. First, I must be assured that what God had recently removed and replaced on my life path with simple instructions to obey were not lost on deaf ears, that the past I endured was not all bad. Yes, addiction is deemed bad by society largely because of the negative behaviors most addicts empower to achieve their necessary fix for the moment. Nevertheless, the self-abuse and the abuse of others is justifiably something to forget, but I say those experiences are the very thing that gave me the strength to face the new path in front of me. I learned positives from those negatives and from that pain had come new growth, like the growth of a flower blooming after a forest fire of adversity to become the rarest and most beautiful flower of all. We, that are here today in that recovered soul, are that flower and we can lead this generation and maybe the next out of addiction. This death sentence brought upon us is worse than in all the years past. I heard and believed that if we don't save ourselves here and now, who will save our children or theirs?

Officer Whitmire and I arrived at the designated courtroom on the third floor with my mind on fire with anticipation and certainty that I had traveled the right path in this program and I had earned my early release. We walked through the double doors and the flood of recognition of what I had changed about myself in six months made some new and old things very clear.

I had started with a new trust in my higher power God. I know I must do, what I didn't do ten years ago when Sister Ann patiently told me when I first met her in that jailhouse program, Pray Daily. I might have avoided much of what I endured had I believed her way back then and trusted it could work. What I couldn't and didn't share with her, in the beginning, was how much fear of God I had and believing no one could ever love me after all the destruction I had done. The long addiction and seizures that brought me time and again to the limits of what miracles EMTs could perform had weakened my mind and made denial even stronger. Mental deterioration steadily wrought an endogenous depression for which women had been given shock treatments and lobotomies but fifty years ago to prevent suicide. What I fully believed was hidden from her view and others was how much self-loathing filled me and how trying to escape the darkness drove the unquenchable hunger for enough cocaine to drive the demons away. I did not trust Sister Ann enough then, to accept her healing medicine to pray daily to be rescued from the vicious circle of doing more cocaine to do more dirty to get more money to get more cocaine to do more dirty, around and around, until I would crash down in a death-spiraling seizure. The unending cycle of darkness I could not perceive engulfing me within the crystalline delusional haze of temporary euphoria where I would stealthily go to capture the elusive genie into my bottle to appear at my command to make me clean. In that unique depression-crazed moment of crack pipe confusion that I prayed not for the happy genie to help me do another trick but to the Holy Ghost of salvation the nun had promised would help me long ago. The fear of an angry vengeful God ceased forever in that eternal moment and a loving God banished the genie away and recovery didn't open the gates of heaven and let me in... Recovery opened the gates of hell and let me out. What happened? Down deep in the fiery burning pit I long suffered needlessly because I did not believe the Lord's messenger until by near destruction I was snatched from the darkness in prayer on my knees. The pent-up anger I held within me that dragged me backward, again and again, was chained and I was free'd. There wasn't much good behind me but there were a few valuable lessons I learned about myself and other people. People can be cruel and cunning with a tender smile, but putting trust in anyone while I was high and strung out could have been fatal like it was for a few I had known. My trust was an integral part of my personal power and I gave it away easily and so cheaply. Never again will I be so naïve.

In the courtroom where I was standing to be judged those insights gained flooded through my mind in a powerful wind of changed beliefs. All trust to be given to anyone begins with that approval that God will give subtlety or overtly when it's right to do I had learned well from Sister Ann. During the ten years between my first introduction to her program and the last, and each of those recovery attempts that I failed so miserably at each time, my failure only happened when I stopped praying. When I stopped praying my judgment soon if not almost immediately, went awry and bad decisions were followed by worse choices. The foundation of recovery that has proven firm, strong, and reliable, is establishing and maintaining daily a trusting relationship with God. This realization and acceptance have proven unfailingly dependable in each step of recovery thus far and I can see no reason on earth or in the heavens, I would ever again fail to pray daily, keep my Faith close and share the message of recovery and God one day at a time.

My once prevalent anger at myself turned to joy that late afternoon when Judge Brown was looking at my achievements, my proof, that I was now fully committed and determined to have a better life. The self-empowerment I had set in motion with daily affirmations while sitting in jail proved strong. Words of self-directed encouragement spoken with a firm belief that I was a good girl, smart, pretty, strong, and capable enough of overcoming all of my life's failures and being loved were true now. This is the place where so many of us as addicts or even non-addicts fail; we give up on ourselves before we give it our true best efforts when they are necessary. Not once not twice but as many times as it takes we persist single-mindedly until we succeed. When we persist and we trust in the right things, a higher power within ourselves once given control leads us to safety in recovery and guides our path. Don't give up believing there is someone inside of you that you can trust with your life. There is and you are the *only one* who can turn the power switch on because no one can do it for you against your will, or without your help.

I stood there at the front of the courtroom in another dimension in time waiting for the Judge to say something and a sudden shift in my reality occurred. A warrior's presence filled me as the new soul in me completely awakened. Standing there in that quiet somber courtroom waiting for my new start, I silently prayed for myself one more time and I promised God that I would share His message of spiritual healing. I could bring Him to life through me to heal the infirmities of those searching for an escape from the big trap of addiction.

The Judge looked up from the thick file in front of him, peered over the top of his half-frame spectacles giving me a quick furtive glance, and then gave the Prosecutor a long wordless stare with a bemused chuckle that bordered on a laugh. He returned his gaze to me and said, "It's my decision to agree to the defendant's request. The case is adjudicated on the basis of time served. Case closed.

You are free to go Ms. Baker."

I was FREE to go!

FREE'D!

I barely held in the scream of joy I was feeling. But I was not without that deep down in the gut and far in the deep recesses of my mind the knowledge in that same moment this was my last chance to get it right. I was on my way tested and proven that I could become an upstanding citizen once again."I can be released now, your honor?" I asked with a sure but wavering voice. "Yes now. You are remanded to Officer Whitmire's custody to complete the release forms required by the Court and the County Jail," he answered looking me in the eyes with a small but perceptible frown and a quick cordial smile.

After a few brief moments of gathering papers and closing a large thick brown file folder, the Judge looked over to the uniformed bailiff that was standing casually against the wall and nodded his head. The bailiff took a step forward and announced matter of factly that "this court is adjourned." I felt the whole world stop turning and go cold silent for a moment and I was a tall grayish stone statue somewhere being watched. The months maybe even all the years of anxiety, anticipation, and fear of being sober and sane again burst open like a dark thunderhead of rain and washed away the grit and grime dross making the statue shiny white. I was a redeemed soul and I was on display for the world to see.

I felt the tension begin to drain from my body as I shuffled along behind Officer Whitmire's fast pace toward the elevators. Down we went and over into the jail where she escorted me to a different cell than I was in before my hearing.

2

Trust and Hope

It was the eve of my 40th birthday, a cold December day in 2002 when God touched my soul with a recognition that could not be ignored. I acknowledged it and accepted my life had been given back to me on many occasions before but the spirit given to guide me forward I had denied the power to do so. I wasn't making that near-fatal mistake again. The Lord was asking for complete surrender to his will and with willful determination, I was committed. I had finally given in and gave Sister Ann, and the

Lord, a small degree of complete trust during the first few days of being within her care again a short six months ago. The spiritual healing began and I was grateful for being given membership into a kingdom of powerful warriors of the Lord. It was a potent blessing with honor and I had much to learn through obedience to claim my true path.

Aloud I said, "Your will Lord, not mine be done." I felt a tingle run through me. Dedicated study day and night of Bible Scripture would become the most meaningful and dependable source of development in the years ahead as His 'will' did indeed fill me!

Awaiting release from a life I never wanted to return to I could feel the hate, jealousy, and anger of those around me who felt trapped in a life they didn't want to live anymore. Could they find the courage inside themselves to change? I sensed hostility surrounding me from the girls in my block that were stuck here. However long it was to be for them it was too long they made clear. I prayed quietly to calm my nerves watching and waiting for the guards to call my name to leave behind this horrible life. I vaguely remembered being almost comfortable here once or twice in the past and that fleeting thought was a harsh and ugly reality of the subtle power drugs had to alter my conscience into happy acceptance of being held a prisoner in a cage. This time my cage became my refuge and a place of rest and solitude to restore me and give me safety and peace that I had not known before. I wanted to be whole and sane and stable as the person I had empowered me to be with the Lord's and Sister Ann's guidance. Rose, a saved and redeemed soul!

Finally, they called my name. I stood up from the cold steel bench and looked back briefly at the jail dorm I had lived in too often over the last ten years. I felt a deep but brief sadness reflecting on all the time I had lost as the heavy metal door with dull gray paint and bulletproof window in it, slid open with a slow crawl. I was Free'd.

I practically ran out the main door and the cold gust of December wind slams me hard. So does my new reality. I am starting over with nothing but a few ragged clothes in a black plastic garbage bag, which represented my entire worldly possessions, and I have no money. Now what? I am free, but how am I going to change everything about my life, from right here on the sidewalk in front of the jail nearing midnight on a cold December night?

I stood there contemplating my choices as the wind bit at my face. A sense of fear I thought I had left permanently on the other side of the jailhouse doors just a few moments ago reappeared. The harsh reality bloomed into painful fullness in my mind of all those countless times I wasted the help offered or given to me! Oh, to take it all back now! Sadness and a new unexpected discouragement began rising so soon after the emotional high of being free to start my life over again. If I had only tried harder would I be here out in the cold with nowhere I knew to go or anyone I could reach out to for help in this first moment of crisis I was facing.

Stop!
I hear myself say.
Today is a new day to get it right.
The past cannot be changed now or ever so let it go... or fail again.

I took a deep meditative breath, and another, and another, as I focused on clearing my mind of negative thoughts. It's only an illusion, the fear is only self-induced negative thoughts I remind myself with positive self-assurance. I had practiced many times as I worked with my life coach in the early stages of the program to direct my energy to positive thinking. I had learned how the power to make better decisions and the follow-through on my choices to get it right worked.

Ok, where can I go right now to get out of the cold? Where can I go to plan the work and work my plan? This simple and short mantra was the starting point, I would start the journey with to solve my immediate needs and avoid prolonging the crisis of thinking and emotions that I was experiencing. I had to stop the fearful or uncertain thinking and take control. Start with the simple and advance along the line to the more complex or larger in a series of small incremental steps. One piece of a puzzle at a time until you assembled them together and completed the picture of the success of your plan. Then execute it with the precision you planned it with adding a little wiggle room for uncertainties that couldn't be foreseen or planned for.

For starters, I need the basics, food, shelter, and clothing. The bag, what's in it? A few t-shirts and pairs of socks, my documents, and certificates to freedom, a cell phone I doubted would work. I remember the bill was always paid in advance for just these types of events. I had lost track as to how far ahead I had paid on it. But maybe it might just work when I needed it most, like right now. Taking it out of the bag I push the power button praying for a miracle.

It buzzed a few times and the dark screen came to life. God was listening! Thank you, Lord, I said out loud. The battery indicator was near zero and I knew every second was going to count. But whom do I call? I have no one to call except those I want to leave behind in that old life, I want desperately to erase.

I felt the cold wind beckoning at me to do something before I stand out here and freeze to death! For a long minute, my mind raced around the question, was there anybody out here anywhere who would answer my midnight call for help? Anybody, anybody at all I wondered? A dim silhouette of a face appears in my mind, a tiny flash of light illuminated Kurt's face for a brief moment. That nice guy who said I could call him anytime. I can only hope he won't regret that now, almost laughing at what I was saying to myself.

Kurt had picked me up one night in the pouring rain as I was hobbling down the street looking to turn a trick and score some dope. I never expected a friendship to grow out of it, but God had other plans that night back in July as a terrible Atlantic thunderstorm rolled ashore and dumped torrential rain. I was soaking wet when he stopped, rolled down his window, and asked if he could drive me somewhere. Before I could answer he was opening the door from the inside and shoving it open for me to get in. I didn't hesitate and climbed in with a big wide smile as I pulled the door closed and thanked him profusely. With a simple 'no problem' he reached around and from the backseat pulled out an old sandy beach blanket and wrapped it snugly around me. He gave me a bottle of water and offered up his sadness and dismay that I was out here in the rain and I was somewhat overwhelmed by his compassion that night. I saw him a few times more and we developed a friendship and I prayed he would show me the same kindness tonight as I stood standing out in the cold outside the jail.

A relationship is described as a state of being in which two or more concepts, objects, or people are connected, or the state of being connected, and is something most of us have no idea how to implement back into normal life. Letting anyone into my world to any degree had proved disastrous in the past. My new skills acquired were giving me confidence that I didn't understand at the moment, but nonetheless, I was willing to trust that I could connect with someone again. We had connected on an unexpected level that night for certain. Kurt had made me feel safe and cared about for the first time in a long time. We had shared for however so briefly something I had to hope would work at least for the time I needed it right at this moment in time, a friend. Someone with whom I could share my feelings and trust that I would be safe once again in a trusting relationship as I fought to put my life back together one piece at a time. I could only hope and pray he did not believe I was just that same street girl who was in a jam now and looking for easy money or a fool to be played.

The phone was ringing and my heart started pounding, 'Hello!' I heard on the other end as the phone slipped from my shaking hands. I grabbed it in mid-air and heard, "Hello is someone there?" I could almost hear the panic in his voice. My hands were sweaty which didn't make sense because it was so cold out here under the stars with a whipping wind and a chill that went right to my bones.

"Kurt, HI, it's me Tiffy" My heart almost stopped beating waiting for him to respond.

"Tiff, where have you been? I tried to find you a couple of times." Hearing him say that I thought, 'wow, he was worried about me.' Almost puzzled by the thought that anyone really cared about me now, a complete stranger really was a new and positive feeling.

"I just got released from jail, and I don't want to go back to that life. Please, I have nowhere to go tonight. I want a better life. I do not want to die on the streets. I want out of that world and drug life. Honestly, I'm tired of it all," I told him with pain and sincerity in my voice.

"Can you please help me until I figure out what to do? It's cold out here and I'm in shorts and don't have a jacket. I'm lucky this battery is still active, It will probably die soon. Will you please come to get me? Please, Kurt." I was trembling from the cold"It's midnight! Why in the hell did they let you out in the middle of the night? That's not cool. Sure I'll be there soon. Try to find somewhere to stay warm and hang up to save the battery."

"Ok. See you soon and thank you, Kurt." I couldn't believe what I had just heard. I could barely believe this man was willing to help me. But I needed to trust in what was unfolding. I needed to believe in this moment and allow someone to help me and follow through with helping myself. I was going to accept his help with confidence and have faith that God's plan always happens for a reason.

I stooped down and huddled as close as possible to the low handrail wall of the staircase that led to the jail visitor area about mid-way up the stairs. I pulled my legs as close to my chest as I could to try to stay warm. Staring up at the night sky full of stars, I saw a beauty that was unseen before. I'm sure it had always been there, but it offered a new and different perspective to me tonight. I felt a new appreciation of the mysteries and magic of a world I had not taken a real interest in for a long time. I had overlooked the simple and undemanding things that made life an adventure to be lived one day at a time for so much of my life. As the stars twinkled brightly in the night sky above me, gentle tears began falling from my eyes and I felt joy and relief at the moment, thinking about all I hoped to change.

As I sat on the steps waiting for Kurt I thought about what might be going through the minds of those who came past me on the stairs every few minutes. No one was laughing or smiling as they hurried along to and from the jail. Staff personnel was apparently making a shift change, but worried-looking family members and friends came and went from the jail in a steady procession that surprised me as it was well past midnight. There was a look of fear and panic on the faces of those hurrying up the stairs and the sadness and anger of most going down. I felt bad for them, in the same way, I was feeling bad for myself and how many times others had made the same trips on my behalf. More so tonight than in the more recent past, I felt sadness and fear mixed together as I thought of how I could mend the relationships in my own life. I had put pain, turmoil, and a mountain of uncertainty into the lives of many others that should not have been there. I had a few ideas to try, but I could not possibly know how anyone would feel any more or how they would react to the choices I had made and the actions I would take as I attempted to start a new life and repair what damage I could from the past, one day at a time. The task ahead of me seemed more than just a little overwhelming with a lot of unknowns sitting here on cold concrete steps with an uncertain future ahead of me. But I would start with asking for forgiveness and hoping they believed in the same God that I did.

I was seriously beginning to shake from the cold and decided sitting here on the steps wasn't making it any better. I knew I had to shift my mental focus from how cold I was and get out of the wind. I decided walking up and down the steps might help me warm up a little and I could review some of the things I learned inside those strong walls to help me navigate my future, my sober life.

I started by asking myself why each Life Skills course would help me and where do they fit into my plan for living in the real world.

Basic Life Skills:

- Taking care of self; being responsible for myself. My short-term needs for tonight are met. Long-term was something I would have to work on; help for Job training, Health Insurance, food, and shelter. The homeless shelter I was in last time was such a blessing; they gave me two weeks to find a job so I could pay my rent. Following rules, accountability to self and others was a big part of it; they had shown me how to file applications for food/health benefits so I could survive on my own.

Anger Management:

- Anger management is the process of learning to recognize signs that you're becoming angry, and taking action to calm down and deal with the situation in a productive way. Anger management doesn't try to keep you from feeling anger or encourage you to hold it in. It does teach you how to feel it appropriately, and this training had already proven effective or LaQuisha might not have fared so well that day in the yard at the jail. Learning new ways to deal with old instinctual reactions will take time to perfect I remind myself.

Relationships:

- Without good communications, you can't have any good relationships. I'm going to ask questions and make expectations clear so others know what I need and want from them and they know what I can give back. An equal give and take, for honest fair exchanges to build trust and acceptance. Practice makes perfect, an understanding to make the little things clear for me and others for the big things to be right. Love just might shine brightly again, one day.

Bible Ministry & Spiritual Training:

- Spirituality is a broad concept with room for many perspectives. In general, it includes a sense of connection to something bigger than ourselves and it typically involves a search for meaning in life. As such, it is a universal human experience — something that touches us all uniquely. As another cold wind rushes against my skin... God wraps his arms around me and lets me know it's all going to be ok. Today was just the start on the path to someday help a lot of people. Trust and Faith in God, I could only pray that to be true. My daily discipline of prayer was firmly set in me and I would not miss my time with the Lord again.

Domestic Violence:

- It is the violent or aggressive behavior within the home,

typically involving the violent abuse of a spouse or partner. But it can be a part of any interpersonal relationship with others. I think about this class and how they taught us to realize we are so much more of value than allowing our life to be lived in fear of being hurt. To never stay in that environment, that the short-term struggles of leaving, far outweigh the long-term abuse. That we all are *significant* and *worthy* of being happy and healthy both physically and emotionally, that *we shouldn't tolerate abuse.*

12-step Recovery Program:

- Where we can learn about its origins, its beliefs, and how its members follow the 12-steps, that described each of the steps in the 12-step program and AA's or NA's philosophy. Tomorrow I would work on getting this set back up into my daily routine, finding a meeting to go to every day; 90 meetings in 90 days, get a sponsor as soon as possible, begin my step work. The last time I got thru the first half of the steps and my life had changed. This time I was going to do a better Fourth Step so I could be confident I know my battles ahead.

Psychology — my theory:

- It was and is in facing the demons which caused our using in the first place, that will help us be successful in recovery, removing the demons we put in place to avoid the real issues. The issues from abuse and neglect, isolation, anxieties left

> ignored and untreated must all be addressed, I searched out this help in my early recovery. Knowing I can face the past for the last time and that my past has no control over me anymore!

The wind was gusting harder but I had warmed just a little walking up and down the flight of steps that led from one parking level to another. Each time I stopped for a few moments the cold penetrated my mental barrier and I began shivering and shaking. I started doubting Kurt was really coming I mean he didn't really know me, right? A girl he found walking the street in the pouring rain in the middle of the night back in July. Letting my mental guard down, I was overwhelmed with self-directed anger for believing that my harsh uncertain predicament could be solved so easily with a single phone call. Discouraged by my limited choices at this moment, I wanted to scream but I knew that would not help me at all.

I knew walking up and down the steps had warmed me a little but it was tiring me and continuing to do it wouldn't solve my dilemma at one a.m. in the morning. I couldn't just sit down on the cold steps and hope that one or any of the few stragglers that were coming or going to the jail could miraculously solve my problem. I had to get out of the cold and wind before the precious energy I had left within me was completely gone. I picked up my bag in a huff and began walking toward the front of the jail complex and the busy main highway. I had walked it north after being released from this same jail in the past to return to the old and familiar streets that had been my comfort zone and my way of life. A subtle but strong impulse of urgency to just accept the pain of failure again and set my will to follow the path of least resistance to solve my immediate problem flashed in my mind. A tear came and I knew more were going to follow if I didn't fight it. Frustrated, stressed, and fearful, I had just given my old addiction an open invitation to drag me back under as the cold reality of my situation lingered for a few long seconds.

The ugly present real-life cruelty that the Prosecutor, the Judge, and my jailers had little if any awareness of was they had released me in the middle of a cold night with nowhere to really go... and no money to go there. They didn't know and I guess it wasn't really their problem anyway to acknowledge my circumstances beyond the requirements of the law. It was my problem, not theirs and they had every right to think and believe they had done all they were required to do and granted me an early release back into civilized life.

A long hard gust of wind raged up and pushed me sideways and I almost fell, but it jarred my thinking away from the remnants of the old life. The old ways of thinking and doing that were oh so easy to entertain for a moment of hope to ease the tension of desperation I was feeling still trying to figure out where I would go in the middle of the night – with no money. Hell-bent on making better choices from here, my mind was trying to stay focused on the task at hand, which was finding a warm, safe place to stay for tonight.

I kept walking oblivious to the traffic moving past me and the curious glances of a few hardy souls walking by and headed somewhere at this late hour determined I would find a real answer and not take an easy and immediate way out of the cold. I heard across the street the sound of a horn from a parked car and then another from a slow-moving car of someone knowing a provocatively dressed female walking the streets this time of night was who she was a hooker. I didn't acknowledge it and kept walking briskly with my head down and ignored the familiar signal of interest in me it conveyed. I forced my thoughts away from how simple and easy it could be to do it just once and get in the car to get out of the freezing cold and get enough money for a single meal. Yes Lord I know you gave me this body and yes I know you helped me get out of jail early to be free again. Yes, I know you don't really want me to be out here on the street alone, cold, hungry, and broke as I rationalized in the past so I could feed my hungry addiction. But you know in my heart and soul I don't want to be that person anymore and that old way can't be your answer tonight. I would never ever be that kind of person and do those kinds of things before I got so badly addicted and weak-minded, I heard myself crying out in fearful anguish.

Oh God take this from my mind, please!

I flinched hard when I heard the sound of a different car horn blow a series of honks and glanced up just a little as it u-turned in the street and honked twice again as it pulled to the curb just ahead of me. I am not doing this I screamed in my mind! I just can't do this! As I approached the rear of the car I saw the window on the passenger side coming down and with a few more steps I glanced furtively through the open window ready to angrily shout out 'go away, go away please!' I turned my face toward the car ready to scream out my plea without losing a step and my heart almost stopped as I recognized it was Kurt behind the wheel in the car.

"Tiffany... it's me, Kurt," he said as if I had not recognized him and was going to keep walking. Though in that paralyzing second the thought had crossed my mind.

Kurt was here to rescue me from myself, a helping hand I was not going to pass up.

The Lord had answered my prayer and Kurt was the proof the Lord had heard and answered that faithful prayer. I hesitantly reached out my hand and opened the door as the surge of emotions climbed. An old familiar feeling, one that now made me feel very uncomfortable, as I didn't want anything from the past to interfere with the present or more so, the future. I climbed into his warm car, lights flashed in my head and I let out the breath I was holding in startled apprehension. Trust and Patience – got it, Lord! I hear the words in my mind telling me, 'it just might be ok after all.' My heart was elated even more than when the judge said 'I was free to go!' A feeling like enjoying a warm, hot fudge sundae snuggled up in a blanket watching a favorite movie again and again filled my happy heart. A lifetime of strong happy feelings collected and condensed into a mere few seconds replacing hours, days, and more of fear and pain.

Those precious seconds were powerful ointments for my cold body and its plethora of emotional wounds and scars. It was good and I wanted it to last forever. But without warning a sky full of happy sunshine I was feeling passed on and gave way to a harder stark reality. My psyche was engulfed by a timely truth, like a dark windowless room with no door out into the light. Or like a long-forgotten music box from my earlier life only vaguely remembered. In it were fragmented conflicts and emotions about the circumstances by which Kurt and I had met before. I did not want to be that girl that he knew from the past anymore or ever again.

I had buried or suppressed my real and true emotions for most of my life. A brutal environment of hostility and physical abuse that I had grown up in required me to find ways to cope with the pain and stresses that were a big part of everyday life to survive. I had learned how, in some mysterious way as an early adolescent, maybe I had learned some of it from my dear Aunt Hazel, to react quickly when it was necessary to contain my emotions and control my emotional responses to others. I had to learn as a youngster why and how to minimize and avoid anger and prevent undeserved punishment from my abusive alcoholic father and overtly aggressive mother against my younger brother and myself. When I was unfairly provoked and needed to respond with any kind of emotional defense I simply kept quiet and defended myself with a wall of timidity and meekness, which was far removed from normal healthy development and the real me. It did however provide me early the insight and instincts to survive in adverse environments. The fault in my plan, if you could call it that or the other, was putting all those suppressed emotions into an imaginary special music box that I kept locked and hidden away that I never opened. On this windy cold dark December night, it suddenly appeared and sprang open.

Most all of those emotions and energy they contained began to flood in on me like a tidal wave rushing onshore from a violent storm displacing the momentary joy and hope of my new freedom and a better life ahead. My true inner self and so much of the past feelings about life and people were tender, exposed, and painful. I was suddenly unsure and more acutely apprehensive about myself. Just how I was going to get the help I desperately needed and wanted this time?

I accepted the innate emotional sensitivity that was my true, unguarded, natural self. I was a woman out in the open vulnerable and could no longer hide from myself the truth of who I was on the inside looking out. I also knew if I was ever to be authentic and deal with the world as it really was on its terms, and obtain the help I needed to fully recover from addiction and prosper, I must be open to new perspectives. Who I was, necessarily could be, and would be had to be made visible to others looking at or into me from the outside.

There was no other way and Sister Ann had made me see the beauty of being the real me. I had to stop being the compliant vehicle for others' needs and wants. Being that had stolen almost all of my life and with it any future that was ahead of me. I opened my heart and opened my ears to my higher power and said a quick prayer the real me could find the human and other resources I needed from here in the dark with nothing.

"Girl, why didn't you wait for me somewhere warm? Sorry, I'm late, but it took forever for the girl to make this. I stopped to bring you something to eat."

With as much etiquette I could muster, given the ordeal of the day and night I had been through I eagerly consumed the OJ and food Kurt handed me. We sat and exchanged small talk for a few minutes in the warmth of the car exchanging brief updates of what we had been doing and what had happened in our lives. I felt safe but uncertain of anything beyond the moment and the plan I envisioned for my future ahead. But there was a history between Kurt and me from that meeting on that rainy July evening and it took front and center in my thoughts when the moment came to talk about it.

"Kurt I need to say something that might not feel right given all that has changed since we last saw each other. I was being honest when I told you I really did want to change my life and I don't want to be that person that I was. I can't 'cause it almost killed me and it destroyed everything that was important to me" I said looking him in the eyes.

"I believe you Tiffany, and I understand, I really do," he said with such caring emotion in his voice.

He went on for a moment explaining that no matter what he truly cared about me and had come looking for me several times to see if I was doing okay. And he made it clear with a few brief but sincere words that he was still willing to help me any way he could. There were some long moments of silence for both of us as the meaning of what I wanted him to know and be okay with tonight.

"Well I know you are tired and need some sleep so let's get going. Do you want to stay at my house tonight? You can get cleaned up and we can decide what needs to be done about tomorrow when it gets here," he offered with the smile that had made me feel safe with him like when we first met.

My future and Kurt's too took some interesting turns and had its share of ups and down's as a one-night stay became weeks and months and into a couple of years. More friendly and platonic for the most part as my recovery began to take shape more fully, we found comfort in being part of one another's lives and finding and sharing the things we needed to grow as adults in a world full of uncertainties and surprises.

The relationship got on solid ground quickly. I had some issues to face and not much in the way of resources to meet them. Kurt made the difference time, and time again with a positive attitude and oh so much support as I navigated the new challenges of steady sobriety and rebuilding the connections with my family members and the few friends who were still around. We shared more than a few upsets without fights or arguments that could have and maybe even should have occurred.

Kurt was resilient and I was willing to accept not everything in my original view of how things would go, did so. There were some memorable events that brought a little sadness and tears but there were far more that produced smiles and laughter than I ever really expected.

3

One of the Good Guys!

Support relationships are going to be critical in early recovery.
I see how in my previous attempts when I pushed help away, I was setting myself up for failure. Reaching out and accepting that helping hand is a good thing, but some of us have unresolved shame and trust issues that delay or prevent us from accepting the

help we need when it's offered. I will talk about the trust issues a little later. Sister Ann had convinced me during our last talk of one sure thing if I walked back out into the world with self-doubt and shame wrapped around me like a coat, just as I was when she offered me her program, not much had really changed.

If I did let go of the very things that had held me in chains for so long, would I be a free woman, a changed person who believed in her future? I wanted to be the person she made me believe I could be I needed everyone to see I was not the same old weak and defeated woman who had given up on herself and given up on life. Would anyone really want to give any of their valuable time and efforts excepting the heavy burden they would be seeing if I left here still wearing that robe of guilt? Her admonition that certainly a minister might want to offer up forgiveness of my sins, but wasn't I in need of something more than forgiveness? Didn't I need to show the world I had taken charge of my addiction and had overcome it with conviction and there was a reason to help me move forward? I believed in her words and I believed in myself now, all I needed to do was engage the solution and other people with it.

A teacher in one of my rehab classes in jail demonstrated how fear and shame sabotages recovery by devaluing yourself and sincere desire in others to make a positive contribution to your success. Holding on to shame is an obstacle to receiving the critical value and benefit others can provide when you most need it. The efforts and resources available from friends, family, homeless shelters, halfway houses, any still willing to help you, is crucial to the process and progress of your recovery. You are your attitude and your attitude is you and both are the determinants of your success or your failure. You are the only one in charge of your attitude so don't fail to let a positive attitude and self-respect define who you are and earn the respect of others whose help you need and deserve.

I finally applied this valuable insight when I stepped out of jail for what would be the very last time. I had spent way too much time and effort packing bad choices and worse decisions into a suitcase and let that outdated wardrobe collect and define who I was for too many years. That wardrobe of shame and doubt was worthless baggage I no longer had the strength or willpower to carry around as 'me' any longer. I left that suitcase on the curb in front of the county jail for the trash collector to pick up when I got into the car of one of the good guys in my life.

I began building a new identity on a new foundation of self-respect that I was more than a sum of my past mistakes. I choose to be an honest and authentic woman who acknowledges and admits my mistakes and accepts the consequences. By doing so and asking others to do so fairly, what I did yesterday does not necessarily determine who I am today except by my choice. I will be tomorrow what I *'will'* myself to become today. I have found a better self-image and when I put it on and wear it, I immediately feel and look better and I am more appealing to others.

My first interpersonal relationship as the new and real me was with a man named Kurt. He took a chance on me standing on the jailhouse curb because he was a nice guy with a heart and sense of optimism about the future. He was not a pretentious person and was very comfortable in his own skin. He was almost six feet tall, short dark hair, and pretty greenish-brown eyes, and a military veteran with a strong physique still well pronounced. His Jamaican heritage became self-evident in his islander's attitude and unique speech patterns. His native dialogues were kind of cool to me and I enjoyed listening to him talk in his natural unguarded way. The Jamaican slang he would sometimes use and his accent made me laugh often. Understanding what he wanted to convey when he was upset over something was an entirely different matter. When he mixed islander words I didn't know the meaning of and everyday English in the same sentence it could be perplexing to communicate, but generally, a few gestures would help me make the necessary connections.

Kurt was sleeping on the couch and I in his bedroom, as he had insisted on day one when he brought me home when I discovered the second week he suffered from PTSD. I thought by this point some behaviors were just not natural. He did the best he could to hide or minimize it. He largely isolated himself from others after being discharged from the military to keep his secrets hidden. In the late '90s and early 2000s, many veterans were coming home from another ugly war with a wide variety of combat-related illnesses and maladies. Some were not outwardly visible or easily diagnosed and many emerged long after separation had occurred. Kurt, like a few others I had encountered on the street, didn't get timely help needed soon enough or at all to overcome a host of unspeakable traumas they suffered. Our government let down many soldiers when their combat services protecting our futures were no longer needed. Many Vets like Kurt were left to self-medicate and or drink bloody images and death moans in their heads away. At a time when Insurance companies did not provide Mental Health coverage or pay for real treatment of mental issues, alcohol and drugs necessarily became the self-directed treatment of choice.

Addiction soared nationwide as the number of returning Vets needing help increased. Many waited months or even years and traveled long distances to underfunded understaffed VA facilities to receive little effective treatment. Only when the President took direct action from the White House after enough Vets and a whistleblower inside the VA exposed the scandalous mistreatment did anything change for suffering Veterans. Too late to help Kurt and many of his fellow soldiers, but thankfully many will be helped today and tomorrow that deserve all that can be offered to repay their sacrifice. Addiction has been declared a medical disease for a large segment of our population and slowly the dynamic of treatment and recovery will change to accommodate the expanded perception of the mind-body relationship. PTSD now has a greatly enlarged diagnosis and treatment protocol that may prevent more veterans from accepting their misery as a sign of personal weakness rather than a legitimate combat injury.

Kurt was slow in revealing any of the traumatic details of his combat experiences and what he did share was just enough to answer questions about some unusual behaviors I probed him about. I did a little book research on my own to put names on things I had no knowledge of. He had a false sense of shame that he was simply not tough-minded enough to control his mental responses to recurring memories of horrific high casualty engagements. He didn't outwardly much blame anyone other than himself and it greatly saddened me he resisted getting what help he could to deal with his personal grief and its impact on his world. This nice guy was willing to open his house to me, a virtual stranger, recovering from a life on the streets where he found me, but not himself to ask for help that he was really owed.

I had to wake him from his disturbed sleep so many nights as he screamed and thrashed violently reliving scenes of human destruction as he helped end the lives of people he deemed innocent of any crimes against others. There were too many ugly events where fatal conflict ensnared innocent victims and the rules of war forced Kurt to choose instantly between protecting fellow soldiers and saving his own life or trust armed villagers were justly defending themselves and their homes from a mutual enemy. Too often for Kurt and countless nameless other veterans in raging firefights they had little control of, friend and foe alike were engulfed in sudden poorly coordinated noisy chaotic encounters of life and death struggle where the good guys were not wearing white hats for identification. Only when the smoke of battle was settled for a few brief moments in the daily procession of death and destruction would you horrifically discover some of those you were fighting for had been standing or crouching in the wrong place at the wrong time. Time and time again the aggression of war day and night drew the blood of a fellow soldier and your own and provoked dark animal instincts for survival. You did as training told you to do. You didn't shout out loud, 'Are you the good guys or the bad guys?' You shot to kill anyone you saw firing a weapon in your direction without waiting for an answer to the question you couldn't ask.

Painful admissions came slowly and sporadically from Kurt that greatly altered my perception of war and combat. I was a girl and I didn't play cops and robbers and soldiers with toy guns as a child. I didn't get heavy doses of TV and action movies that portrayed the sights and sounds of war that males so often did growing up. I learned little by little something about the ugliness of fighting with deadly weapons and the dark sights and sounds of humans dying in armed conflict. With pleas and occasional demands, I appealed to Kurt's need to let go of shame and guilt hoping to defeat some of his demons and free him from a prison of despair.

The first few days and nights away from the confines of jail and its routines were challenging and uncertain when Kurt's personal realities and routines were added. He slept at night with music blaring so loud it was almost deafening to me. Drowning out the noises in his head made it possible for him to sleep but almost impossible for me. It was the only way he could sleep at all then and I was a grateful guest and I didn't want to be a problem for him. I was willing to do anything I could in exchange for his willingness to help me and determined I could find a solution to this problem that worked for both of us. The loud noise of guitars and drums and wailing vocalists overpowered to a degree unforgettable sounds of brutal up close intense warfare. The first two nights I simply put a pillow over my head to lessen the effects and slept fitfully for a few hours. By the third night, I had decided I would lower the volume a tiny bit each time I awoke from a brief sleep and see if he reacted to it. I did not get a full night's sleep the first few weeks there, but I had decided I would have to get the real sleep I needed when he was away at work during the day. Thus I managed to navigate the first obvious obstacle to being his house guest amid his personal nighttime demons. Night by night over the next few weeks the volume went down to a bearable level for me and seemed to be working for him and allowed me to sleep a lot better at night foregoing multiple daytime naps.

This horror show going on inside Kurt's head was not so unlike that of others who for varied reasons struggle with unresolved physical or emotional conflicts or trauma. For the most part, I believe they all do want help to deal with or overcome the conflicts but lack the necessary trust to allow it. I had been that way myself for most of my life not knowing, believing, or simply doubting anyone who could help me really wanted to especially once they peered inside my head. The sadness in my heart grew as I began to understand my own dilemma better and saw and felt the pain of self-doubt and isolation that Kurt experienced as a way of life too. I wanted to change that for him and I thought I could take a chance, a small tiny experimental step for both of us, and maybe, just maybe, it wouldn't shatter the delicate but mutually beneficial relationship we had built so far.

I believed and planned during that first full day of freedom the stay at Kurt's would be only a few days. I did not do all the things I did to get myself straight, free from a life where my body was a tool to be used and abused to support my addiction, to let my future be anything like the past. I had pledged to myself it would be a long time before I would ever be casually intimate with any man if I ever was at all. I had grown enough mentally and emotionally to know there were so many expectations and entanglements revolving around intimacy of any kind that could shatter my future I simply would not let it happen. I was determined I would do what was needed to secure my independence as a single person and live alone somewhere and have a new life that worked. If the right guy happened along who could accept my past and meld with my family I might try being a wife again, maybe. That was my plan.

I honestly and for good reasons saw myself as being 'at' Kurt's rather than being '*with*' him when I arrived to be his house guest. We did have a relationship of sorts previously in which we were intimate, but we had mutually agreed before we pulled away from the jail, that sexual intimacy was not a condition of our agreement to help me. But the days turned into weeks and then months became the new unplanned reality. There were more unknowns and unexpected problems to solve than I had visualized from the inside looking out than I anticipated. Navigating them one by one took a lot more time than I thought they would and each day it became more apparent it was going to be much more difficult and time-consuming for me to become independent and self-sufficient than either of us had expected.

No significant conflicts developed between us when new roadblocks appeared largely because Kurt was a naturally patient person and did what he could to lessen my frustration with soothing words of encouragement. We both enjoyed our time together and I enjoyed the quiet security I had while he was gone all day at work and neither of us got overly distressed our original plan had changed quite a bit. Continuing the daily work on my success plan and overcoming obstacles my past created and getting my life back in order was being mutually shared in a positive way. It was going to be much harder than I had originally thought, but we were both determined I would be successful and it would happen and I would move on and out into a secure and stable independent future. It was always just a few more days or a few more weeks… or so we believed.

I contributed every day what I could in a practical sense and to not be just a burden in Kurt's life. I cleaned and scrubbed, swept and mopped, dusted, and polished his apartment top to bottom inside and out. It felt really good to do things to show how much I valued having a secure place to be day and night and make his life just a little bit better too. He wasn't a slob but he wasn't a neat freak either so the efforts I put into it he readily showed his appreciation for with big smiles and thank you. He never made me think or feel I was a burden or an intrusion and said he was happy to have someone to talk with and share the everyday routines of life with. I felt the same way. I wasn't a problem he had to solve and his attitude and his actions made me feel like a person he was glad to know and be with on an everyday basis. This helping hand and gentle soul God had brought across my path was helping me deal with old wounds and new challenges and gave encouragement I needed to displace anger born of fear and frustration. Being in a safe place with a self-secure man allowed me to find and begin nurturing a part of me taken long ago when marital vows and bonds were shattered by repeated infidelities and a slow steady intentional destruction of my self-worth. I went adrift for ten years of life as a numb empty emotional shell. I began feeling those little positive emotions again when my daily efforts to make Kurt's world a little better yielded unexpected admiration and respect he didn't hesitate to show. It was new for both of us to be in a harmonious relationship living in the same house with the opposite sex that was completely platonic. I wasn't unaware that there were some occasional natural urges Kurt felt and we would have to deal with this soon because my few days had become a few months. Yes it was a big comfy couch he was still sleeping on and I did remain respectful and admiring of his chivalrous pledge being okay with me finding my new personhood while sleeping alone in his bedroom each night, but nature was still nature and it would have to be addressed soon if I was here too much longer.

The platonic relationship we were maintaining seemed to be working for both of us. Simply making sure the house was clean and his laundry was done made for a good partnership. Kurt was a "Chef" and oh my, did his clothes reek after a night in the kitchen. I did have a few dark flashbacks relative to this during the first weeks there that reminded me of my first job as a teenager in a restaurant with a leering predatory male boss who I knew given the slightest chance would have sexually molested me without hesitation. I shook off the ugly memories each time and believed Kurt would not reveal a bad side unexpectedly and shatter our peace.

I remained for a long time hesitant about trying to cook for Kurt, but I truly loved learning as he cooked for us daily and I watched with genuine interest while he did. Chef Kurt enjoyed teaching me his culinary secrets and his unique ways of expanding simple dishes and it was therapeutic for both of us.

He treated me as an equal and didn't subdue or subvert growing strength in me as a whole person free from being a fearful overly submissive woman. I was free from my debilitating addiction and identity as something I never ever wanted to be. The woman Kurt was seeing each day was a real improvement and I was not only recovering what was lost but creating something that was new and better than I had ever previously been.

I would be a hypocrite if I believed or said that being an attractive single adult female under the same roof with a single good-looking virile adult male day and night sharing a close friendship wouldn't naturally create some sexual tension at times. That Kurt and I had been casually intimate twice some years ago added to his dilemma given the explicit agreement we made sitting in front of the jail that sex was not a condition to staying at his apartment. Neither of us at that point foresaw me being there more than a few days or what direction his gesture of human compassion would take us. Yes, there was some conflict arising and not so subtle anymore, his positive approval was something I naturally responded to and by now I kind of wanted it too. It was the things I was doing automatically like you do when someone does something extra special for you and it makes you feel warm and fuzzy and you say a sincere -Thank You!- with a big appreciative smile... and sometimes a hug. It's just a natural response. Those natural responses between a man and a woman can make for some awkward and fragile moments when you are trying to maintain a platonic working partnership like we were. I guess it was easier for me than him because I was not only having no sexual thoughts whatsoever knowing the disastrous realities it had created in my past but also because I was fully focused on being recovered without any dependencies on others to be ashamed of. I fully realized there was a problem when non-sexual well-meaning hugs I gave him a week apart apparently led him to believe that I wanted or was at least willing to be intimate with him again. The result both times was a readily observable silence the following morning when I said goodnight and climbed into bed closing the door behind me and went to sleep. Things went back to normal with us a day or so after each time as we refrained from more than small talk over dinner about the day's events and watched TV until one or the other decided to go to sleep. But, I accepted the responsibility that my approval-seeking and non-sexual displays of affection were a potential threat to our stable platonic relationship and I refrained from saying or doing anything that might cause Kurt male distress or lead him to believe I wanted to break our agreement and be intimate.

I worked on the NA steps with both heartache and joy. I went to meetings and worked with my sponsor Ruth, an old biker chick that was hard as nails on me. She pushed me to work on the steps emphasizing I had to do a thorough fourth step, and it would allow me to face many things I had not yet addressed. Making true and lasting amends to my family was my next major hurdle. There was a purpose beginning to grow within beyond just being a woman freed from emotional and sexual abuse, addiction and an illicit means of supporting my habit, and a turbulent life on and off the street. Regaining my lost identity as a mother to my children and hoping they would once again accept me as their mother and all that could go with it was my biggest challenge and priority. I wanted each of us to know the true joy and happiness of regaining something lost and be there for each other as we grew something good and lasting from the disarray that alcohol, drugs, and marital infidelity had unleashed. I wanted to be a steady source of care and concerted actions to assure my children I wanted to make a difference in their lives. I had begun our shared journey with real optimism; they would soon know without reservations I wanted and enjoyed being there for them as they grew, and being the mom I was supposed to be meant everything to me. I knew it could be difficult but helping my children understand what happened to me, and understanding from their point of view what they had experienced during my absences, was central to my reasoning and plans.

I continued to stay clean and do everything needed to sustain my personal growth. Reaching out to God first, I prayed daily and studied my Bible and other spiritual books Kurt had given me. I worked diligently at enriching my life with whatever was available. I got a library card and began reading and studying with an open mind any material I thought could improve me and make my journey ahead and Kurt's, less uncertain and more productive. I knew and accepted my past was full of negative people and experiences that limited my interpersonal capacity to engage the world without a lot of personal distortions. Sister Ann had convinced me I had a severe blind spot and it was going to be up to me to understand how that blind spot affected my future and what I could do about it. I was not at all sure to what degree my personal beliefs, formed from life thus far of abusive relationships and self-directed social rebellion that was my street life, was going to impact my future. I could only do what I could to continue the process of rebirth and resurrection from personal destruction behind me. But I was seeing strong fresh sprouts of a successful and independent life emerging from the dust of the dead life I no longer lived.

I had made plans with Jared to spend a day with the kids at a park near their home on a Saturday morning and luck made it a beautiful crisp spring day. We found a long table with a canopy near the big oversized swings and unpacked a picnic lunch and a pair of kites the kids hoped to fly. A day of questions and answers, play and laughter, a picnic lunch, and getting to know each other again emerged and blossomed into a happy day for us. My fears turned to joy. "Mom come and push me," twelve-year-old Johnnie shouted out again and again. The sound of his excited happy voice calling to me, and the emphasis he placed on "MOM" making us aware he wanted only me to push him brought tears to my eyes that day that was hard to hide.

Crystal, my almost sixteen-year-old daughter, stayed close and attentive all day choosing to be near over happy frolic. She had serious girl things on her mind for my ears only and she had questions she dared only whisper to me. When seeing my sudden tears she didn't expect she asked with wide-eyed alarm, "Mom what's wrong!" I replied with the biggest heartfelt smile within me, "It's nothing sweetheart, mommy is just so happy to be here with you, come on let's go, I will push you both on the swing." She ran out ahead of me, seated herself proudly on her swing, and beamed a broad eager smile awaiting a big push.

"How high can you fly?" I asked with mock uncertainty as I pushed her hard. Johnnie kept yelling 'push higher mom, higher' each time I switched over to his sister. And push I did, back and forth, pushing and launching them up and away to the limits the swings would take them until my arms ached. After they had flown in their arcs enough to wind them both, we switched to twisting them up tight in the chains and letting them unravel spinning round and round until they were both too dizzy to spin again. We had lots of fun that day and it really felt as if I had never gone away. Nothing had broken the bond between natural mother and child it had only flickered a little maybe but that special day it revealed itself true and strong. I could not only feel completeness emerge that sunny day as it replaced that tiny gnawing sensation in my head of missing something, but I could see it as well. My children, the man who helped me create them and bring them into our world they called dad, and even though he had thrown me away, the four of us were a whole family on this day. My broken world was reformed and it felt right. Even though I knew Jared and I could never be together as we once were it didn't matter. There was a completeness to know and I saw my world taking on new shapes and colors, having feelings I truly thought might never return, life in recovery was awesome. We ended our day together only when darkness came. We hugged and kissed and said our goodbyes closer together than we had been in a very long time.

Kurt came and picked me up before he went to work and I gave him a brief recount of the day's events and unleashed the tears of joy I had mostly held in while I was with my kids. He was happy that I was happy and I gave him a hug and a quick kiss on the cheek and thanked him for all he was doing not just for me but for the sake of my kids too. He smiled and told me to keep my faith it would all work out soon enough, just be patient. For that night and many days and nights ahead I focused my mind on the ways I would remake the personal relationships that had been damaged by my addiction and the years of neglect they suffered.

The biggest thing yet undone to do was asking for forgiveness, then accepting that forgiveness and completely believing it by those who meant it. "Of course I forgive you because all I ever wanted was for you to be happy and healthy.

This is what I think most of us strive for in our recoveries. It's critically important to accept early in recovery that some of the people we will ask to forgive our actions, just can't find it in them to forgive us. There will likely be for you as there was for me the one or a few who say the words to you and try to assure you they are true. But you will know just as I did, the words don't carry the power you feel when someone who means it says it. Trust me if you don't already know this reality; there is a power you feel in words of forgiveness spoken honestly and truthfully. Unless your mental faculties aren't fully detoxed you will '*Know The Difference*' between simple platitudes and true forgiveness is spoken and meant. I know just like you should and must, we have done our part to get clean and we are engaging fully in our recovery plan including trying to make amends where and when we can. But beyond any and all doubt, holding on to any guilt for what you simply can't change, immediately sabotages your recovery and defeats your higher power from advancing you along your path. I learned by Sister Ann consistently illuminating the power of guilt that defeated my true strength and produced the longest relapse in my past. Guilt leads to doubt and doubt leads to inertia and inertia makes you vulnerable and susceptible to using again. Don't dare own the Guilt.

This part of our step work in recovery is hard but the sadness of recalling it is necessary. Focusing my mind and transcending into a dream state, remembering all the ugly things I had done during those bad years, and then revisualizing myself standing on a tall mountain waving goodbye as they faded into the distance was a cleansing ritual I repeated daily for two months to work through the painful cleansing process.

The guilt and shame of letting so many people down was a bit overwhelming and I feel a lump of sadness well up in my throat and felt the tears begin falling. I quietly speak to myself, 'today I will forgive myself.' Accepting that I can't change what happened but I will keep my word now. I discovered for myself how slow the process of self-forgiveness can proceed, and that it may be the most difficult part of recovery. It would be very true for me.

Kurt was finding new little ways to make me aware of some powerful but subtle changes in my personality. The frown I wore almost continually that reflected my fears and distress because I was overstaying beyond the few days we had planned, had been replaced by a near-constant smile because I was contributing beneficially to Kurt's daily well-being. The harsh self rebukes spoken about the harm I had done to my children were replaced by positive things I was doing and would do. He didn't see from me angry responses to repeated rejection or prolonged wait times to access resources I desperately needed, I smiled with a quiet firm determination saying I will have to try something different tomorrow. His attitude and his emotional support were helping me grow personally and proceed on my recovery path to do the work required. He also pointed out I was making his life, less isolated and stressful. I had no false impression or illusions I alone could do much toward relieving him from the terrible PTSD that can leave soldiers scarred for life. Knowledge gained from the books the library had relative to PTSD was just enough to reveal treatment and recovery for him would be long and was best left in the hands of trained professionals. I could help him most by letting him talk when he wanted to and assuring him he was not alone. There was help available to him in the present that wasn't there earlier and he could benefit by sharing with his fellow veterans and help each other.

Kurt was an amazing chef. Cooking was the one thing that gave him peace and little temporal jolts of great pleasure. With a slow methodical sampling and balancing of individual flavors, he created unique tastes to create culinary dishes that met his very high and narrow expectations of perfection for me. Three, four, even five hours he would be in the kitchen on his days off the first month I was there. I sat on a stool in the small kitchen while he explained how achieving the flavors he wanted were all about cooking time and temperature and there was a perfect time to combine them with other parts of the dish he was preparing. He just relaxed and smiled and talked about food and cooking. How he learned to cook, discovering some very unusual meat or vegetable dishes, or how he had thought of unusual ways to combine different dishes into a meal, all of them were fascinating to me. Simple things about foods and flavors at first and then he would talk about exotic presentations he had created and what people said about them. Native foods from Jamaica were his specialty and they were very popular in the better places out on the beach. He was very proud of his Jamaican heritage and always smiled when he talked about the people he grew up with and how most of them always wanted what was cooked by his mother and how that made him a lot of friends.

The few hours we saw each other in between his shifts and the one or two days he was off work each week we watched TV or talked about my future. It was maybe my third week there when we decided on his day off that week to walk together to the market to assemble another of his exotic food feasts. I was surprised when he started talking about himself. We spent most of our time together so far when he wasn't working mostly talking about me and my future. The various things I wanted to do or didn't want to do, how soon it could happen, and all the little things that might be important to some aspect of my recovery. Positive things about how well I was doing each day with particular things, or who I needed to talk with to get help for some problem I was foreseeing. It was light and casual chatter and heavily interspersed with sports and different teams we liked or for him and followed avidly.

   Kurt surprised me on an early morning foray to the food market choosing to talk about him as he rarely did. To and from the market, about two miles from our apartment, he revealed how different things were for him before and after his military service and how it made him feel about getting close to anyone now, man or woman. The time we shared together that day was the only day he would talk about his personal feelings, his emotions. By the time we had cooked, ate, and cleaned up, I understood why he preferred being at home alone rather than being out with the guys on a Friday or Saturday night. But maybe the more meaningful thing to me still stressing about how long I was being there, was hearing him say how good he felt about being there for me when I called him from the jail. He told me with sincerity being there was medicine for his soul and I relaxed my fears just a little and thanked God for His mercy that Kurt answered a strange call in the middle of the night.

   Finding trust again in another person and believing I wouldn't be abused or neglected physically or emotionally was my greatest need. Kurt's few words that day were the calming my soul urgently needed, someone to just be there for me with no demands or strings attached. It was extending beyond my planned stay with him and it did bring an unexpected shift in my thinking, and now I say it was more my feelings, from 'being at Kurt's to 'being with Kurt'. It was the first of several shifting perceptions that we were approaching a different place in our relationship that might pose a real threat to how I was seeing my future, the one I believed Kurt was seeing also. I wasn't entirely certain any longer I knew what he might really want to happen if I let it. I wasn't going to let it happen. In the past, I did let it happen when a frightened, unsure, naive female, fresh out of detox in her first weeks of outpatient treatment living in a women's halfway house, let those fears lead her into a plan with another ex-addict to 'have a future together.'

Our foolish plans, largely composed of our mutual overconfidence and real-world thinking that was still distorted so soon after detox was at best a house of cards. The 'We' failed quickly when my Prince Charming went out for cigarettes, got high, and left me holding the bag of failed plans with little money and no one to turn to who wanted to help me. I relapsed soon thereafter and found my way back to the streets to do another tour in hell as Kurt called it when I finally told him about it one Sunday over dinner. I was working towards independence and my own place with Kurt's help. We had begun our arrangement with my call from the jail, to leave my past behind me and we both knew what that meant without putting it all in words.

We proceeded along on our spoken and unspoken promises to each other as old and true friends who cared deeply about the well-being of each other and would help each other achieve their goals. It was honest and it was simple.

Kurt was happy he could give me time to focus mostly on my recovery but he showed me often he also enjoyed not having to come home to an empty apartment after a 16-hour day in the restaurant kitchen. There were nights we barely spoke as he showered, had some food, and then stared through the TV, trying to relax from the pain in his feet after standing all night. But he knew that I was safe here while he was gone all night and I was beyond grateful for the time to put my life back together, preparing for the day I would leave to be on my own again. The quiet days for self-directed growth he gave me is something all of us need to make the small steps required to recover our identity and plan out our path to follow. I truly believe two people in any committed relationship need sufficient self-focused alone time to secure their relationship as a partnership of equals with individual perceptions and unique contributions that make it a happy and productive union. Kurt and I gave that to each other in a steady and predictable manner.

Things just kind of coasted along for a few months and there were a few bad nights for Kurt when an unplanned triple shift to help out a coworker happened. He went almost three days on his feet and just a few hours of fitful sleep on the couch before he went back to his regular schedule. I tried my best to get him to sleep in his own bed the three hours he was home on the third day, but it remained my bed in his mind and he didn't want to disturb my sanctuary as he had started calling it. On the fifth day, he finally came home a little before midnight, took a shower, and crashed onto the couch with only a few tired words exchanged. I turned the music on for him at a level high enough to keep me awake but I hoped it might help him get clear of the agitation he was clearly experiencing. I went to bed leaving the bedroom door open and listening for any noises that meant it was going to be one of those bad nights for him.

Maybe it was an hour maybe a little more, but I had dozed off and was startled fully awake by a loud scream and a flood of shouted words. I jumped up and took a few long steps to the couch calling, "Kurt it's okay, it's okay!" I kneeled down beside him and repeated the words over and over until he jerked awake and looked at me. "Oh God, Oh God, Oh God!" He began jerking and began trying to force himself deeper down into the couch and I grabbed his hands and repeated his name firmly and calmly until he stilled and looked at me with wide-open eyes. A few long minutes past our eyes locked together while I knelt beside him holding his hands tightly telling him I was there and everything was alright. He squeezed my hands a little harder and said in barely a whisper, "I am sorry Tiffany. I'm okay. I didn't mean to scare you. I really am sorry."

"It's alright Kurt. You didn't scare me. I was awake reading and I heard you make a funny noise, so I came out to check on you," I happily lied with a reassuring smile as I let go of his hands and stood up. It was the least I could do to make him feel a tiny bit less ashamed, but I felt in my heart it wasn't really enough. It didn't feel right seeing him alone, fearful and uncertain that it really was alright and he really was okay.

"Kurt, come on get up, go get into your bed. You need a decent night's rest in your own bed for a change." He resisted and pulled back for a moment trying to maintain his vow to avoid any and all things that might break our sincerely meant agreement. We had both become more cautious to avoid arousing any romantic thinking or casual joking about anything sexual. I was not feeling anything sexual but it felt totally wrong to just leave him to go back to sleep on the couch wondering if a worse night might be yet to come.

I reached down and took his hands in mine and said, "Hey we are big kids. Don't worry we just need to get you back to sleep so you can get some rest for what's ahead tomorrow. We will be just fine. It's really going to be okay I promise. Come on get up." He got up slowly without a word and we walked to the bedroom and got into the double bed I had been sleeping in alone for the last several months. It didn't feel wrong but I wasn't sure it was right either. In my half-awake state of mind, I believed it really would be better for him to sleep in his bed and get the rest he desperately needed, and I could shake off some of the guilt I was feeling for leaving him on the couch for so long instead of me. We were both in pajamas and I figured we could handle being in the same bed for a few hours under the circumstances. He fell back asleep after a few minutes and soon I heard a gentle snore and I turned on my side and put my arm across his chest and fell asleep feeling it was okay, we were both safe here together and trust meant a lot to both of us.

I awoke in a slow and hazy manner sensing it must be morning and it was time to be awake and get up. It was a tiny brief shock that I was not alone in the bed before the memory of Kurt falling asleep beside me returned. Yeah, it's okay I remember what happened. I opened my eyes and saw sunlight streaming in around the sides of the window curtain and turned my head a little to find Kurt wide awake and looking at my face with a beaming ear-to-ear smile. I couldn't suppress the automatic warm response of "Good morning!" We had slept a few good hours safe and secure in our pajamas and yes my hardy hero had gotten some sleep I guess. I had done the right thing and he had returned safely from the scary battlefield in his mind and I smiled my approval that he was here and I reached out to find one of his hands. I squeezed his hand looking into his eyes and saw reflected not masculine desire but honest admiration for my act to comfort him in the dark. There was a quick flicker of understanding exchanged between us somewhere in our minds or maybe it was our souls that said all was well. We had both gone far in a few short months accumulating an acute understanding of what each other was thinking at the moment and laughed often when we easily finished each other's sentences. Mutual little insights and perceptions of our mental workings were revealed unguarded with trust and confidence.

I had rescued him temporarily from another nighttime firefight and put a barrier between him and the faceless enemy he couldn't control for a few hours of peaceful rest. The wall we had put around my femaleness with honorable intentions to secure me while leaving behind forever that other woman drugs had made me could not stop the warm strong feelings flowing through me in a new day. Being deeply cared about by a man again, and this man an old fashioned gentleman more akin to a knight with a strict code of chivalry, than a hardened war veteran protecting us from the world and our own unguarded natural impulses, had genuinely committed himself to my well being without any strings. I raised myself up and leaned over and kissed him softly. Yes, it was alright this close together in a big bed and I would be safe in his embrace if he wanted to hold me close and join his heart with mine. I didn't believe I had to resist the naturalness of being this close to him anymore. My heart was beating faster and harder and each breath shallower as Kurt pulled me close and held me tightly to him. I uncurled my body and put my arms around him and squeezed him with all the strength I had.

We crossed our strong-willed and well-intentioned boundaries we drew when I was shivering on a cold December night sitting in his car. A lot had happened since that night and we were not going to change what we felt being together now after being intimate again. There were anticipation and excitement planning a road trip and an adventurous week at Disney that was as close to a real honeymoon as I had ever known. There were the long weekends spent at Busch Gardens or in Daytona for Speed Week. The months flew by. We went to Disney again with Kurt's family from Jamaica and had some good old-fashioned fun. We spent a lot of time closer to home at the beach, swimming, and surfing in the warm Atlantic Ocean and having BBQs to hang out with my kids. Christmas came and went again, Kurt always making sure that I had something to give them for birthdays and holidays, just a small loving gift for each of them. He was my superhero now and I wondered how I could be blessed with someone so loving and loyal.

There were plenty of simple pleasures we shared on our weekly trips out for groceries or thrift store treasure hunts. We walked or sometimes cruised in the car following signs to garage sales talking about the neighborhoods we were in and the people we were meeting at each stop. We grew our relationship talking about what the future might hold if we stayed together or I did as planned and became an independent woman. Pro's and Con's about our own individual choices and what did it mean if we stayed together and just kept going as we were. Enough trust and time had passed that disagreements weren't quickly avoided and a few significant conflicts arose largely because our pasts were so different. We had not done many of the same things when we were kids growing up or teenagers exploring the world around us and our place in it. His years of calm, steady, and stable were vastly different from my stormy and turbulent home life of isolation and fear of recurring abuse living within an extended family of alcoholics.

There were enough common beliefs about the rights and wrongs in the world and we agreed things should be better but knew it was less likely every day. We laughed about life moving too fast and nothing lasting as long as it should and people being in too much of a hurry to get somewhere or anywhere but where they were. We didn't at the time glimpse a covert implication about that belief and the unavoidable reality it applied to each of us and our relationship. The revelation was largely overshadowed by our new and temporal romantic and idealistic expectations. Remaining a couple, having children together, melding our families, following a normal and socially approved dynamic of developing and maintaining a few strong friendships, and nurturing a family culture of optimism and adventure about the future was the journey to our destination. Yes, for our own unique reasons we both wanted to believe within our reach for the taking was a storybook progression of the sinner to saint, failed pursuit to ultimate victory, love lost and love found, happy endings if you dared believed the dream and made the effort. The secret we didn't know was the mystery of which book we believed in as our story. Kurt's natural life-long optimism about things, in general, had displaced some of my latent fears and mistrust of people's motives, but observation and painful experiences had taught me to be cautious about happy illusions and promises they might empower.

4

Stepping Stones and the Fight!

Kurt and I joined minds and efforts rebuilding my life stability within a few days of my arrival, but everything took time and I was starting at less than zero. I came out of jail with only a state-issued I.D. card. I was starting my paper identity and life status over again with less than nothing. Everything had been lost, stolen, or sucked into the drug-clouded vacuum of life on the street. There was a certain amount of incredulity, and often a wariness that I was who I proclaimed and wasn't running some kind of con or scam they had not encountered before. I didn't make sense to them. It perplexed almost everyone I spoke to on the phone and almost always those I encountered in person face to face, that I was not a recent immigrant. Yes, I had an address to use at Kurt's but that was only days, a few weeks, or a couple of months old. Just where had I been before and what was I doing they wanted to know.

And that was how many years ago? They repeated as if they misunderstood my answer the first time they asked. Oh... you were homeless for ten years? Oh. Well, okay, just a minute please, I need to talk to my supervisor about this. No Social Security card, no driver's license, no insurance card, no credit cards, but I did get a library card on the first try because the silver-haired retired school teacher turned librarian listened to my story and believed I was 'such a nice young lady.' I signed up for all the help I could get, food stamps, school, health insurance, and my Social Security Disability... again! Getting my food stamps enabled me to share in keeping Kurt and me fed and I felt less dependent and a burden on him. Trips to the market to gather ingredients for my next cooking lesson forced but enabled me to end the avoidance of people and relearn old and new social skills I badly needed.

Returning home from the markets one afternoon I asked Kurt, "Can I try cooking the curry chicken and the red beans and rice?" I laughed at him as he gave me a goofy look before he replied, "Of course, I'm right here if you need me or have any questions." I started my first adventure in cooking for him just as I had observed him do many times. Bake this for so long, boil those, simmer that, add those slowly, stir, stir, wait, and a few minutes pull it out, and then there it was ready to plate up and serve. I had learned a little bit of his kitchen magic. And honestly, his ear-to-ear grins and laughter while I put our dinner together, was oh so good for my soul. I never believed myself the greatest imaginative cook, but certainly, now I was feeling like something of a chef if only for a few hours.

When we had finished my culinary feast his simple but meaningful "Dinner turned out great Tiff, guess I'm gonna have to let you cook more often," made me believe we might have made our humble little apartment a home. I smiled ear to ear, laughed at him, and said, "We'll see."

It was a satisfying state of mind being with a man who was more attuned and genuinely interested in who I was mentally and emotionally rather than what I could do for him sexually. It was a relatively new experience for me and I couldn't stop being a little apprehensive remembering I had felt something close to this during the brief courtship and the first six months of my marriage to Jared. He too was warm and very affectionate and wanted to know what I really felt emotionally about most everything he said or did and he would make any change that made me feel more loved, important, and happy to be with him and he assured me it was forever. Jared, who rarely could be at ease just enjoying the simple everyday things of life. After we married Jared was always living in what tomorrow was bringing and it was where he made so many destructive mistakes for us. Kurt lived in the moment of today while Jared lived to satisfy his yearning today for what he hoped tomorrow would bring.

My apprehension in the relationship with Kurt now centered around how quickly and without warning, things turned upside down with Jared. Overnight he replaced asking me to do something with insisting I do it now, receiving or getting approval or consideration for acts of love and care I freely gave him required showing him I was actually worthy of his praise or efforts first, and affection he replaced with dominance and near-constant sexual demands that were physically painful and often degrading. Almost overnight a loving kind man became a sexual monster with an insatiable appetite. I wasn't sure that Kurt might not be somehow the same and not be who I thought he was. I shifted my thoughts away from the disturbing differences and came back to the happiness of today.

Crystal had done something sweet for me after she had gotten permission from Kurt and bought me a Lovebird, naming him Sweetpea. Sweetpea loved to fly around the apartment, sit on the edge of the fish tank, drink water from it, and generally provide me something more to fill in the everyday routines. At just sixteen Crystal got her first job and with her proud earnings, she bought me this present. It was a huge thing for both of us, and each day I am given a reminder of her love when I hear Sweetpea talk or sing. I was concerned about some of the issues she was having that I learned of through Jared or Jared's new wife. Crystal was more and more focused on things she said she didn't have or wasn't getting and she was constantly displaying her dismay at everyone failing her. She had frequent bouts of screaming rage that expressed more than anger and was akin to getting revenge on those she said were neglecting her. We were each stunned by her outbursts knowing that she had everything she ever asked for and was given more freedom and independence than most sixteen-year-old girls. But clearly for her none of this was enough. Jared and his wife Katie made it clear to me one day when Crystal adamantly refused to come with Johnnie and spend a few hours together with me at an amusement park. She raged and stormed and made it even clearer that day with her words and actions the daddy's girl expected the world to take care of her and she refused to believe it just doesn't work that way. But even though Jared and his wife and I were on the same page about this and tried hard going forward from that day to show her that it was not to her benefit to act out this way at the slightest of provocation, we remained largely unable to get her to see her own fault in her thinking and actions.

I was extremely grateful for my new friend Sweetpea and happy to have him around to keep me company. Did you know that lovebirds actually make a purring noise when they are in a very calm state, it was the funniest thing the first time I heard it. I would learn later it was true of all lovebirds when I received another lovebird someone had rescued from neglect.

Kurt enjoyed our thrift store shopping, it was a way for him to get away from his work and let his mind wander looking at treasures that once belonged to others. I knew he insisted we do it regularly to get me out of the house and keep me engaging with new people. We had been looking for a few weeks for some specific furniture but mostly browsing for the fun of it. On a wet Saturday morning, I happily remember it just felt different. I was feeling some very strong feelings about how far I had come from being in a cold gray jail cell following the only routines prisoners can do and how much freedom meant. We stopped browsing and I stood outside a storefront and said, "Thank you, Kurt, for all you have done I hope you know how very grateful I am." Looking down at me with a happy tear on my face and gently wipes it away and told me, "I do Tiff, come on let's go find you a new bedroom set."

We went inside and began searching the rows of furniture and I spot the perfect one. The salesperson had been following close and noticed me looking around the store for Kurt who had gone off to the other side of the store. I wasn't leaving my new treasure was all I was thinking. Steve, the salesperson says to me, "Well is that the one?" I giggle a bit and say, "I supposed it is if the price is right. Did you see where my boyfriend went? I want to show it to him but I don't want anyone to get it first." Steve assured me he would go find Kurt and suggested I lay down on the bed and give it a test run. A few minutes later the two of them returned and looking down on me lying on the bed Kurt asks, "Are you sure that's the one you want?"

"I love it, it's beautiful can we afford it?" I ask. The excitement in my voice and the expression on my face must have been huge because Kurt put his arms around me and said, "You know I love you right." I totally busted out in tears of joy and said to him, "I do."

After we got everything all worked out, I just stood there

glowing with a new level of happiness reveling in what we had just done together for me. Steve told Kurt to back the truck up to the loading dock out back and I'll have my guys load it up for you. Kurt asked him how much to have it delivered because we didn't have a truck.

Steve said, "Well it's normally fifty dollars but I'll do it for twenty-five." That sounded okay and Kurt thought it was fair too and the only question remaining was when they could deliver it. Steve checked with his delivery driver said it could be delivered the following morning. We thanked Steve for his generosity, left the store, and exchanged a lot of happy smiles and even a strong high five on our way home. I hardly slept that night anxiously awaiting the morning to come and waiting to see the truck pull up was a big step up for us from the ten-year-old double bed we had been sleeping in and a rickety chest of sticking drawers with a cracked mirror. When it finally arrived I finished moving the old stuff out of the way that Kurt and I had not moved before he left for work and helped the delivery guys get everything put in just the right place. I thanked them profusely and they were on their way and I began dancing around my new piece of heaven. I felt like I had wings on my feet making the new bed just perfectly and putting our clothes and things in the nightstands and the big mirrored dresser. I was a queen in her castle.

The smallest bits of emotional compassion can sometimes dramatically change a person's world. Kurt changed mine as a woman with his actions of the heart that day. He gave me something very special and I am forever grateful. We had reached a very unique level in our relationship because I had never experienced the kind of equality we shared and neither had he. The continuous give and take and the subtle search for a balance that kept us each giving on the exchanges of care and consideration, and to the degree, we thought we understood 'love', we had found harmony for however long it would last.

Daydreaming one afternoon after doing some studying, I began thinking about what it was going to take if I wanted to have my own apartment again. How would I get the furniture I needed, the appliances, all of the things I had at Kurt's, and maybe a few other little things to make it unique and special. What about work? I had not punched a time clock or set a schedule in a while, and what kind of work could I do and where would I find that job? Waitressing with my bad arm might not work so well. My heart sank a little and more negative images appeared on my mental roadmap to a happy future. The hard facts of more physical limits my injured body imposed and presto — self-doubt began rearing its ugly head. Really? Really? Must I accept that I can't possibly do it all alone and I will always have to be dependent on someone for my care? I won't! I absolutely won't accept that as my fate! Fierce anger arose in me for letting the first seeds of self-doubt take hold at all. Satan... hit the road. My past addiction and my old negative beliefs are not going to win this time. I am much better prepared with those anger management skills firmly embedded in my mind like a blinking caution light that says 'Slow Down'. I calmed down, made a new list of exactly what I needed, how I would get it, and where I was going to be in the near future. I would not be defeated.

I had believed getting my disability check from the Government would take no time at all and I would have a way to pay my rent, buy some new clothes, get a phone, and lead a stable life that my teenage children would be a big part of. Nothing happened as easily or as quickly as I had expected it to. It seemed at times futile and no one I was talking to or working with seemed to have the right answers or know anything different than what I did. I was impatient which led to fear which lead to frustration which led to more doubt but all the time my steady discipline kept me on my feet knowing I was not going to quit. Some days became high-speed emotional roller coasters. Good news at 9:30 a.m. and bad news by noon. Another round of phone calls reaching out for help at 1:00 p.m. and being told to call this person or that but all I got was recorded answers we are away from our desk or on the other line or with another client... but leave your name... ad infinite for days, and then weeks, and then months, and sadly yes it went like this for almost four years and three appeals before progress was finally made and my disability claim was approved. A major battle was won but the war was not yet over. I learned one very valuable lesson from the continuous daily struggle; how easy it is to give up and fall down again. I experienced some discouraging tear-filled days of self-doubt because I finally had to accept I would never again be able to do any real 40 hours a week physical jobs again. I was disabled for life to some degree but I didn't give in to depression and go find a fix to soothe my pain.

But on the recovery path, I saw or heard about so many in the smoky rooms or at treatment centers who did. They had oh so sad stories to tell about how hard they had been working and how much they had done... before they gave up in sight of the finish line. Pity.

If we tell ourselves at any time before we succeed at something it's going to take too much work, we have already miserably failed. I had done that and had given up on myself one, two, three, four, yes.. five times too many. That pity party was over, the enablers I had always invited to my party had been sent away, all the banners and balloons were taken down, and the trash that was my weak-minded moments of self-pity were gathered up and thrown away. The moment you take to stop and feel that seemingly acceptable little bit of pity for yourself, it best be because you didn't finally succeed sooner.

'Winners never quit and quitters never win' was the first mantra I adopted from the little Power of Discipline book I left the jail with. Kurt wasn't pushing me to leave and though he was okay with me being there with him I felt terrible about the extra burden I had become in his life. It took almost 4 years before I ever received my first check and could give him any kind of financial help for his years of personal sacrifice and the sincere acts of love he had given me. The harmony of our relationship had taught me much of the real 'how to' of honest and equal interpersonal relationships, something I had not acquired in the long series of dysfunctional relationships that were my history. I think I learned a little about trust and being trusted with the human heart and all that can mean. We both did what we thought and believed to be fair to each other. We built trust in what we did much more than what we said. We each learned to communicate our feelings, our values, and our needs and wants, better and more often than we previously knew how. We discovered by sharing the things that made us sad and the things that made us happy without keeping silent or keeping secrets we could better understand our differences and accept the consequences they ultimately had ahead for us. Letting someone help me was a big step but one I knew I couldn't avoid sitting in a cold jail cell I wanted to leave and never ever return to. Overcoming my fear and pride to reach out to that helping hand of a man that was reaching for mine was what ultimately saved me.

In the years with Kurt, I used all the time I was given to relearn who I really was before and without the drugs and rebuilt myself emotionally and physically. I utilized everything I could find to propel my life forward; there was no rock I did not turn over in my quest to become the person I wanted to be. I shared often at meetings how important it was to take the time in a safe place such as a halfway house to grow, follow those rules and find that job and stability needed to have your new life, much like the safe place I had. Telling them as often as I could stick it into any conversation, what an utter fool I was to have relapsed and thrown away those repeated chances. There was no hesitation in openly and clearly stating it was only by God's grace and obedience I was here today after surviving multiple overdoses and three near-death experiences.

Kurt had spent his spare time driving me to doctor appointments and surgeries, which included a seemingly endless supply of questions and answers about my life. I survived the poking and prodding into my physical abilities and pain levels as they evaluated and cataloged all my injuries while having to relive all the events over again in my mind. I rattled off explanations of how each one happened, how each injured piece of bone or torn muscle and ligament or tissue reacted to pain brought on by something as uncontrollable as a rainstorm or the cold of winter. All they could really do was listen, tell me how and why to follow the guidelines for my medications, and warn me about the consequences of not doing so with great emphasis. I was blessed by all the good doctors and people I met along the way on this recovery journey. I showed sincere appreciation and gratitude to everyone helping me deal with the reality of the life I now had to endure. I learned to enjoy what I had the best I could and grew ever more determined to find the straightest path to a satisfying life with family and friends. It was just ahead of us or me and I would continue to do my part.

I engaged myself in the couple duties needed each day and used time beyond that in study or in prayer. I worked on things that demanded a lot of my time and attention early in the morning such as the government's protocols required in order to qualify or maintain the help I needed. The X-rays & MRIs that had to be recorded, the exhausting reports and multiple doctor visits to go to, getting the blood drawn and tested to allow pain meds to be prescribed and monitored. Drug tests are done to make sure that only the medications and levels the doctors prescribed were passed. Nothing else was of any importance to me during those times as it was the solid foundation I needed to stand on. But unfortunately, I had progressively gotten worse physically as the long-term effects of my abuse were clearly taking their toll on my body. I tried to walk as much as I could by going to NA meetings not far from where we lived at a little church or swim in the pool at our complex if the weather was favorable. I kept my mind busy working crossword puzzles, word searches, and jigsaw puzzles that were framed, now hang on the walls in my office. I did anything I could find to keep me focused and growing.

I often surprised my sponsor when I was working on my fourth step. She was only vaguely aware that I had reached this level a few times before but had relapsed and threw away all the progress

I had made multiple times. I had so much shame bottled up in me I really don't know how I could physically move. I finally discovered the true source and cause of my descent into mental destruction and addiction. It requires fearless honesty and it's the core of your program and it can place formidable emotional obstacles in your path. You must willingly step into it to conquer it by taking complete control of it. But the truth is the growth and esteem building therein can sustain you against some hard blows to your self-image that make you feel you just can't do it, the heart-wrenching pain you might experience is just too great to continue the battle. But that's why you have a sponsor if you are on a successful recovery plan, being there for the crisis of self-belief that you can go on and conquer the demons that are really just ghosts to be banished. You and I are more powerful than they are, we just need someone to make us see it and believe it. This is the core of your program and the crossroads to getting well or running from the issues back to addiction.

Peggy, a friend in the program at the little church close to our apartment, was a few years older than me and was also doing her step work and wanted to know why it was so damn important. She asked me, "Tiff why do we have to go through all this crap? It just makes me angry, and then I want to use."

Giving her a very assured look with a smile I replied; "Listen I know what you're saying and it sounds like the safe way to go by avoiding it, but if we don't face these demons they will eventually drag us back to hell for a visit." She looked at me kind of strange and then laughed before nodding her head in agreement telling me she would see me next week at the meeting. I always looked forward to going to meetings and making friends and acquaintances to hang out with. It was a careful, slow, and steady process moving beyond the tight boundaries of my comfort zone with Kurt and the little apartment I had made into a calm little retreat from the world for the two of us with the Lovebirds. I kept an open mind at meetings because I had realized I had formerly walked with blinders on and had developed my own brand of tunnel vision. You don't realize how alone you can make yourself without a lot of effort. Addiction is that way. It blinds you in small steps, or maybe even a few big steps for some of us, our perception becomes narrow and we force-fit so much that is gray into simple black and whites that completely distorts our view of the human condition we are all a necessary part of. How many times my drug-shaped perception led me straight into another year of hell and another until the distance back was too far to travel with what little was left of my mental and physical capacity. I can only agree with one of my truest and most trusted ministerial friends about something he believes firmly, "Obviously the prayer you mumbled with that tiny bit of submission faith you retained from those parochial school lessons hidden in your head somewhere was heard. Think maybe God laid you down dead in the dirt that hot summer day and gave you a new soul a little less rebellious?" I could reflect on this when I see others on the street or in a smoky room at their first meeting looking like zombies and I tell myself, "There but by the Grace of God, Go I."

Still working on getting my disability, the infuriating Disability Lawyer Simon I had to hire after the 2nd year and third denial of my SSDI benefits (Social Security Disability Insurance) was a real jerk. Arrogant and pompous he was a little man who really could care less about his clients or helping them at all. He was clear about the fact he did what he did, for the money he was being paid if he won the settlement. He also didn't want to put in any real work beyond the simplest matters of my case, which was much less clear-cut than those he usually accepted, he made clear. He liked the easy cases; like those left hurt by doctor negligence or a car accident, possibly a work accident, those easy clear-cut cases that no one was going to question. Mine was filled with ugly questions and remarks and I began wondering how many more times I would have to answer them without any progress being made.

I think the horrid little man had a barely repressible disdain for women in general but most certainly the glaring look and repetitive use of *'prostitute'* or *'prostitution'* or *'hooker'* gave him some kind of sadistic pleasure that he willfully used to belittle me and make me accept I was beholden to him and I should happily accept it.

I had to do a vast majority of the work required myself. I began to realize if it was really to succeed it would largely be my own efforts rather than Simon's. Working with this jerk wasn't easy but I was determined to do whatever it took to secure a better life. There was no rock left unturned, phone calls made, or paperwork and medical records gathered up and then sent off to this jerk of a lawyer so I could get an appeal set and another chance to see a Disability Judge.

Simon never believed in me or the case.

Fighting for my life's stability would lead to a whole lot of repetitive probing each time a new hearing was obtained. I had to prove beyond any shadow of a doubt I needed and was worthy of any help or assistance I might get. My first Disability Judge, who only saw an Ex-Addict with a criminal record, a broken woman, simply assumed the class of people I had 'willingly' hung around all those years made me deserving of my condition. I was sitting at the table in a cold room and I was visibly trembling.

The Judge asked me to raise my right arm.

As I did, he had said; "Oh you're not disabled, see you can lift your arm. Denied."

Again! Really! 'Seriously are you kidding me,' I thought to myself unable to respond to him.

How did being able to half raise my arm constitute being able to function on any level at the work I had previously done over my lifetime. Years of waitressing, or being able to carry or use the tools it took to fix computers, electrical lines, or the countless other things we all need to be able to do to function in the world! I could barely close my fingers around the handle on a gallon of milk and lifting it to waist height without dropping it was out of the question.

Nevertheless, I was not taking 'No' for an answer.

Winning my case was the only answer for any long-term financial stability in the years ahead of me. The reality was I would only become more crippled as I aged because getting better from these injuries was just not going to happen. There had been too much damage to my body physically by the assaults endured as a child and teenager and out on the street. So with all the will and belief left in me, I pushed Simon to take my case all the way to the appeals court, filing with the Baltimore Social Security office. I would sadly struggle another long year proving why I would not ever be able to work again in the fields of skill or trades that I worked before addiction finally took me down.

Three plus years of adversity and struggle strengthened me in ways I could not foresee when I left my past behind in the suitcase on the curb in front of the jailhouse. Whether it was the Lord's grace, Sister Ann expanding my perceptions, Kurt's military experience, or all of them and my own last chance to get it right attitude, I had learned the value of discipline, <u>self-discipline</u>. I was never a lazy person and I liked working, but I couldn't work a regular job when I arrived at Kurt's, and that hurt me emotionally and physically. Along with the New Years' wish, I made at Kurt's just a scant few days out of jail, was My New Years' vow, to become independent

A small mini-book pamphlet was given out in one of the jail programs I completed titled:

"The Power of the Disciplined Mind"

I read only once but I had kept it and packed it in the black plastic bag of worldly possessions I left with. It became a well-used recovery resource for me and I reread it the second week I was at Kurt's. I memorized some of the key phrases and they became my 'Focus Mantra's' for learning self-discipline. It was a springboard to rise above the real danger of an idle mind in an ex-addict. I had always liked learning new things and I liked to read and I had time during the day while Kurt was at work to do the meditations and mental exercises.

There were no empty or unproductive hours in my life day

or night after that. I got that library card and expanded my understanding of self-discipline and applied it every day thereafter. I planned the work and worked the plan and tracked every objective from start to finish on paper. Everything I had to, needed to, or wanted to do, was done to a schedule and an objective. I pushed myself mentally and physically every day to expand my mind and improve my overall health and be the best partner I could to Kurt.

There were benefits to achieving an even higher level of discipline for the body and the mind. Even though I had physical handicaps and was limited in the types and amount of time I could engage in physical exercise, the routine of walking every morning rain or shine put me in a positive mood. Step by step, I extended the distance until I couldn't take another painful step. As the routines set in and became automatic self-disciplined responses to the sun being up, I started reaping the benefits. There were days I absolutely couldn't walk for reasons of severe pain from the weather. But the impetus to do something productive with the time was automatically there and I did other kinds of muscle exercises I could or did something else on my Objectives list. My entire self-discipline plan was stepped up each time I was denied because I had to consider that I might be permanently denied my disability status and I wanted to be prepared to do whatever I could to be in the best physical and mental condition I could be.

Kurt was always complementing the changes and shifts in my attitude or behaviors as a response to my steady self-imposed discipline. He was always a beneficiary in some way and he understood I was always focused on lessening my burden on him or improving his well-being in any way I was able. At times he would go through periods of saluting me pretty frequently and then he might shift to saying 'yes sir' or 'no sir' or 'reporting for duty' or some other equivalent usually with a big grin or a laugh. As time went by I wasn't always sure whether it was meant as a positive or negative.

Our relationship was becoming less predictable than it had

once been. I was full-time busy steady growing and enlarging my mental world and not certain every day that the relationship Kurt and I had was on the same level. We each were working at self-improvement, me in occasional outpatient treatment and meetings, and he had gotten into a VA program I found for him for Vets with PTSD. We didn't spend as much time together for a variety of reasons but it really wasn't anything I thought harmful and there were indeed a few dramatic changes and a lot of small but nonetheless significant shifts in our feelings close to each other. The relationship wasn't bad it was just different. I thought some days in simplest terms we were outgrowing the old basis of being together and there didn't appear to be anything ahead to replace it. There was no longer the intensity of cooking a great meal or finding that special something at the thrift stores we didn't much go to anymore.

I suppose I should illuminate because it's important to any relationship building in the present tense, most especially for those in any kind of recovery, that intimacy or sex can never be a foundation for a lasting relationship. Men and women are very different in their beliefs about sex and relationships. For the one, it's physical for the other emotional and beyond that, it is extremely personal and unique. A real relationship is built on everything but sex may be an oversimplification but it is largely true. I realized Kurt could not shake off all the aspects of my past or his somewhat mistaken beliefs about it. I have never known or heard any girl or woman say she enjoyed sex, in sex for money exchange. Some men and I found out only too late that Kurt was one, believed that somehow a woman enjoyed sex in the sex for money exchange. Somehow in the beliefs they had, the female hooker had some kind of foundational desire to be always interested and willing to engage or perform any and all sexual fantasies a man could possibly imagine. Inferring because they had worked as a hooker surely they must have willingly engaged men in all of those fantasies if they were paid enough for their services. None of those assumptions are true but the myth is so pervasive and so powerful a perception about working women I think it hurts almost every woman because the belief is still so widespread.

Gentleman and Shining Knight Kurt was slow to fully internalize and accept in his thinking I had used my body *only* as a means to support a ravenous addiction. I had told him so painfully many times. Because the addiction was so powerful and my mind so dysfunctional I simply resorted to being a working girl because it was the only avenue I had to escape the ongoing destruction that two addicts in a marriage were producing and to feed my own habit. There was never even one day during my time on the street I wasn't getting as high as I could just to be able to go play the working girl role... so I could make enough money to get high enough to blank out from my mind the revolting things I just did to get more money to get high and do revolting things, ad infinite, on the addiction hamster wheel.

I was a normal female before the childhood rape, a boyfriend with nothing but sex on his mind and I a naïve teenager, and a monster of a sex fiend who emerged six months after I married him, kind of distorted my natural beliefs about human sexuality. So no, sex did not become what Kurt might have expected it was going to become between us. I enjoy sexual intimacy in all of its normal modes and means of being expressed. I am not a prude and no my abuse on the street didn't destroy my capacity or enjoyment of all good sex can become between trusting caring partners. But I was never nor could I be a wild no holds barred and no limits are known sex addict ready willing and able to go farther than any woman you will ever know and at your command. Even if a man had an unlimited amount of money I always maintained reasonable boundaries no matter how high I was. It's just the way I was wired thank God. So I say that all too pervasive myth about hookers and sexuality hurts us all as normal women because we are simply normal. I like normal. Don't try to build a good relationship or let someone else believe you can on sex or sexual expectations.

Sitting on the couch late one morning with sunshine gleaming through the window and I was thinking about the mysteries in the Bible and how to understand much of the spirituality I was reading. When Kurt walks up beside me and hands me a small stack of books.

"Here Tiffy. I know you are searching for answers to some questions and these might help" he says. I take them from him and examine each one carefully.

"Are these about God?" I ask. The smile on his face warmed my soul.

"They are about *spirituality* and other ways to perceive the same enlightenment and power of a spirit filling you with all the good you can manifest. Take your time and read each one. I have read them each more than once and each time I gain something new from them," he told me.

"Thank you, Kurt, I appreciate them very much, and though I do know about God and Jesus through my church upbringing, I am unsure how to tap into a real feeling about God or a higher power as they say in the rooms," I replied.

"Well Ms. Tiffy, I think these will help," he said before walking back to the bedroom to change for work. Returning from the room ready for another long grueling night on his feet in that hot kitchen, he asked me. "Tiff, what day was it you said that next doctor appointment was?" I told him, "Oh it's Thursday morning, but I can take the bus if you need to rest. I do know how little of that you get already." Smiling at me again Kurt replied, "No hun, that's not how this is going to work, I'm with you thick and thin as you deal with all this stuff, no matter what it is, I'm here for you."

I gave him a huge hug, kissed his cheek, and said to him, "Have fun in the kitchen tonight and try to get someone to help you with inventory tonight." Looking down on me as he stood almost a foot taller he just said, "if only that could happen."

5

The Therapists Couch

> who you were,
> who you are,
> and
> who you will be,
> are
> three different people

The thought of therapy or talking to anyone about my feelings or my life's tragedies was something I was not highly motivated to do at first. There was shame and secrets packed so tightly into the safety of the ebony-colored music box in my mind that I dared not open it even a little because they would all flood out over me at once and I might be crushed to death. I had been forced to fill the shiny little box to overcapacity little by little as my life unfolded and bad things repeated time and again and dark tragedies had to be hidden away forever to protect those I loved. I could not let the pain they were come out into view and be remembered by me or known by anyone lest the burdens of guilt and blame drive them away leaving me more alone and helpless to stop the sad music we would all endure.

My little wooden music box of memories had once been real, a gift from my sweet Aunt Hazel when I was just twelve. It was dark glowing ebony wood trimmed in bright gold with a tiny lock and key to secure the box lid closed and keep the small drawer it had secure with small treasures or jewelry that I was expected to acquire in the years ahead. Opening the lid activated a little matchbox-sized spring-driven pinwheel underneath the box that played a fifteen-second metallic sounding tune like an ice cream truck three times or stopped automatically when the top lid was shut. It was lost forever when Jared and I were forced out by foreclosure from the home we had bought before the power of our drug use left us temporarily homeless.

Ironically years before when I was still in high school I had read a story as part of an English Literature class assignment about a young woman with a beautiful red music box her male suitor gave her as a wedding present. Her beau tragically died a few days later the day before their wedding. She kept the precious letters he had written to her during their courtship in the music box and she never married choosing to live alone with her memories of love reading his letters again and again until her final days came. She was tired and weak, bedridden, blind, and passed on hoping she was leaving to join him in the heavens with her mental music box open playing its tune while she clutched tightly his love letters in her hand and his love in her heart.

I was moved by the tragic romantic story and had gotten the idea a few years later to have my own music box in my mind that was the real music box Aunt Hazel had given me. I had no love letters for the box to hold but the spinsters' great strength was the power in my box to contain the sad pains and dark secrets that it must hold hidden away keeping me safe from dark memories.

A patient and unthreatening therapist slowly convinced me after a few weeks of mostly dull and superficial sessions my past and my pain was safe with him. I carefully explained how I found a way to cope with tragic events and hurts and things I simply couldn't deal with by hiding them in a small magical music box, I had in my mind. Thankful for finally beginning to trust that he could help me to resolve some of my many conflicts, he urged me to share the meaning and purpose the music box had if I could. I would travel back and forth through time with Doctor Pat and Doctor Stella's occasional suggestions and prompts guiding my treatment sessions to understand how unresolved conflicts and traumas shaped my life and they needed to be brought out of my music box to be examined. I hesitantly agreed and we began a journey into my personal hell that I had locked away for a very long time.

I opened my music box cautiously a tiny bit to illuminate my hidden secrets that were my life before, during, and after my addiction. I had filled my music box with horrible events, painful disappointments, and sad memories, and all the secrets it could hold. The bad things began replacing the good things it held at seventeen years old a few days after a brutal physical exchange with my drunken father had left me bruised and in shock.

Lying on my bed in the dark later that night the memory of the spinster's story arose in my mind as I tried to find peace with all that had happened that day. The ultimate trip to the floor reeling from his slap to my face had been preceded by days and nights of him drinking and brooding about things my ma had done or not done while he was away for a month on the road trucking across the country. No, I knew she hadn't had an affair or been unfaithful in some way but he feared she had. He had not seen the proof he wanted that it hadn't happened yet or wasn't always on her mind. He openly expected to come home one day to find us all gone. That is what I gathered from his cursing and bellowing for several days and nights when she was there in the house trying to calm his liquor-fueled fears or as he paced around the house mumbling angrily to himself while she was away at the grocery or running simple errands.

My mistake, if it was one at all, happened on the third day after his arrival when I had come home from my waitressing job to find him hollering at my mother huddled on the floor. I had seen it so often before and knew he would continue his attack on her till he either beat her senseless or he passed out, raging and red-faced when blood pressure and alcohol exceeded his limits and he fell on the floor or bed. I felt a sudden cold fear when I got close enough for him to see me and I saw his eyes narrow to dark little slits and he said with a force I felt in my bones, "You need some learnin' to you little witch! I know what kinda woman you gonna be too if I don't straighten you out right now."

He jumped at me raising his arms with hands curled into fists and I ducked from his path and ran to my mother hoping I could somehow drag her away from the hulking menace I thought might kill her this time. I had grabbed her arm and screamed at her to get up – get up when I felt his first blow to the back of my neck. I wasn't going to let this happen was all that was in my mind and I grabbed her limp arms with both of my hands pulling when he grabbed my shoulders and pulled me away from her as I screamed at her to get out of the house. I instinctively pushed my body back into his unleashing the force of all the repressed anger and rage from years of repeating these ugly brawls. The unexpected force of my body colliding with his propelled him back a few unsteady steps still clutching my shoulder with one hand in a crushing grip dragging me unsteadily backward. He fell on his back and I crumpled down onto him. I knew I had to get up and get away to get Ma out of the house quickly. I twisted away and was on hands and knees facing him and he turned on to his side and swung his hand too quickly for me to avoid a stinging slap to my face that sent me sprawling backward and I toppled flat again.

I was stunned by the brutal force bringing tears and a spinning in my head and a sick feeling in my stomach made me begin retching violently. I forced myself up enough to puke on the floor instead of myself and stayed there on hands and knees shaking and too dazed to move until I felt another urgency that he was going to start attacking us again. We would be dead before the beast ended his murderous rage.

I don't know how long I stayed there on hands and knees before I saw him across the room on the floor not moving. I was wobbling and sobbing loudly and the burning acid taste in my mouth and throat and something flowing from my nose filled my senses. My face throbbed and my body ached and I couldn't get my body to move at all for fear of falling on the floor and being sick again. Minutes or hours may have passed before I finally crawled to Ma and could see in the dim light the blood under her nose and the discoloration around her left eye. She was breathing slow and steadily and was not dead as my first impulsive awareness of our reality made me think she could be. I felt the quick jolt of relief that she was in bad shape but she was alive. I could only wipe away the last small tears I had cried and say out loud to her and myself, "It's okay. You are going to be okay Ma, we're both okay." I stayed beside her my wet hand stroking her still head until a flicker of horror flashed in my numb mind. Oh God, where is Mikey!

The sudden fear pushed aside everything else in the dark world we were in on the hard wooden floor and I forced myself up and half ran to Mikey's bedroom calling out his name. I opened the door to his room and went in and knelt down beside his bed and saw he was in it holding his favorite stuffed animal. I put my head close to his and listened for a long minute. I heard the steady rhythmic breathing with the sound of a plugged nose that told me he had fallen asleep crying during or after the ugly battle that had started before I came home. I finally fell asleep totally drained and exhausted sitting on the floor leaning against the bed with one hand on Mikey and one on the brown stuffed dog with the big button eyes that was mine before I gave it to him years ago to comfort him after another fight played out and left its mark on each of us. The event was the first to go into my mental music box for safekeeping.

I put there for safekeeping many tragic events and emotionally or physically painful memories that happened before I received Aunt Hazel's box at twelve years old. One by one I reached back in time and collected them and carefully placed them in the box. Slowly but steadily the box got completely full and could hold no more and maybe for the same reason my life almost had to become less full of fear and anguish and pain and I closed the box one last time.

There was much secrecy and shame in my childhood. More was added as a willful teenager became a young adult and fled an emotionally destructive hell of a home life, found a career, got married, made babies, got hooked, and got lost in addiction for more than a decade. Let's venture back to Texas and my youth living in that house with a monster of a father and a mother too scared to fight for us and too weak-willed and fearful of the unknown to grab my brother and me up and flee the abusive tyranny we were suffering.

A state of fearful anxiety that began soon after my birth grew steadily transcending any power those few who saw and acknowledged it had to alter any reasonable part of it. My extended family was with only a few exceptions various levels of functional alcoholics. A few of the females only drank a little, but my relationships with them were strictly controlled, by my mother. Hardly could I share with anyone the truth of so much of what I experienced. My mother was so affected by the power of appearances and deceptive self-perceptions about what others thought or might think of her, she was neurotically delusional. We were warned time and again about anyone at all getting even a hint of what our real home life was that might conflict with the falsehoods she openly proclaimed we would be sorry. I was too ashamed to ever let the few friends I had known ever come to our house. Too often we were sorry as she would leave us completely unprotected from his harsh abuse without provocation.

I saw how weak she was when she denied physical abuse she saw happening with her own eyes and I was punished for disagreeing with her that I deserved a slap or a punch in the gut from my raging father. She never went to any extremes to punish me for implied infractions of her strict controlling attitude and demands that made me responsible for many of the household tasks that she should have been doing herself. There was plenty being meted out by my father for no reason that it was utterly unnecessary to even raise her voice. I feared her cunning way, which I did not want to emotionally accept was exactly that until my therapist all but forced me to twenty-five years later, of extracting punishment from my father in her absence to maintain my cooperation or silence. It was entirely taboo to reveal our discomfort or tell the truth about bruises and scars that anyone would notice or question us about. It must have been absurd to some relatives and family friends as we aged to hear the total falsehoods we gave that 'we were just playing' to explain injuries that I and Mikey had received from fists, feet, belts, broom handles, or a chair that was thrown once.

The worst for me as a female was being unable to tell anyone about the molestation and later rape by my cousin Pete. I knew fully Ma or Pa would refuse to believe me as they did about so many other things they knew and denied and they would punish me for 'telling such hateful lies about your cousin Pete. He is a good boy and you know he is.' Pete's repeated threats about ever telling anyone were done with fists raised and in a manner so threatening and emotionally severe and distressing it would be more than two years each time before I could keep the events out of my everyday thinking. Later Jared added his emotional abuse and sexual perversions to bring about a psychotic break reaching the tipping point and my descent into a deep endogenous depression. Ultimately more years would have to pass before I overcame the fear of revealing any of the events and seek help to overcome the demons that haunted me nightly and sometimes in broad daylight.

One of my earliest therapists, Dr. Pat had told me that rebuilding this part of my mental self was critical. I remember him telling me that getting over rape especially when it happened as a child was not going to be an easy task for me and that I should not be afraid to share any of the anger it would bring forth as we moved through the process. I shook my head in understanding and sat there for a minute debating with myself if I truly was ready and capable of opening my music box of pain and be free of the psychic disarray that it had created. I decided it was now or never if I had any chance of my wounds being healed and I truly wanted to be a whole functioning person and with Kurt waiting at home to help soothe my fears and encourage me to maintain my steady discipline of recovery, I was going to go forward into the unknown.

It was both horrible and liberating to endure the week-to-week stumbling daze it became for the self-illumination of my step-by-step descent into the mental darkness and despair that was me in the raw. It was at times as nauseating as the worst roller coaster ride you could imagine and just as frightening. Taking each piece of me out of the music box and recounting and reliving the times and places and all the colors and sounds of my distorted emotions and the unreality in which I was existing and surviving often left me numb for two or three days. Recalling and recounting some significant events while I was married to Jared I discovered and understood the power the first line of cocaine had to begin the dismemberment of my reasoning capacity while believing the drug's powerful euphoria made it mostly harmless and I believed I could trust Jared as my husband and protector. But the opposite became true as I rapidly lost all power to defend myself from both him and the drug.

Once after a prolonged coke high and discovering Jared was steady having sex with other women while I was pregnant something in my head and my world broke. Jared had me committed to the hospital Mental Ward and one of the first doctors to examine me wanted to know why I refused to talk with anyone. Why I was sitting and just rocking back and forth? She also wanted to understand what kind of abuse I suffered from my husband. Jared gave her some bull crap story about why he had brought me there. He had help from others who were making huge sums of money off our business and they had Baker Acted me into a mandated stay until the doctors felt I was not a danger to my young children or me. I just couldn't form words to speak but I could vaguely understand what they were asking. It took almost ten days before the anti-depressant meds they gave me began to rearrange my mind and I could speak and loosely make sense of the world around me. They diagnosed me as suffering from a severe Bipolar Manic-Depressive state and put me on high-dose Prozac.

Another doctor, a psychiatrist I presume today, informed me that I would have to converse with her and tell her what was going on with me so she could determine when I could go home and until I did I had to remain in the hospital for an indefinite time. I spent the first few days there quietly sitting in the large atrium watching other patients with illnesses and maladies of various kinds make it through another day. Some sat still and were completely silent lost in their own minds and I believed they were never going home. Others were crippled by the pain of memories or hallucinations that tormented them relentlessly throughout the day. I watched quietly as orderlies moved about pushing wheelchairs or wiping up spills from outbursts brought on by bouts of sudden rage in their minds as they sat helplessly strapped to oversized wheelchairs. I remember how so many came and went through the atrium that looked just like me who seemed to be simply enjoying being pushed around or wheeled through on their way somewhere. I slowly began to believe I needed to get out of here but I really didn't want to go home and be around Jared anymore... but what about my babies.

During the next few sessions with my doctor in the psych ward, I explained to her that my life was a disaster. Everything I had worked so hard for over the last ten years was now gone and that shutting down inside had crept up on me slowly after I became pregnant last year. She asked me what kind of career work I did. Why had I stopped working? Finally, her last question was did I resent my new baby who kept me from working?

I explained to her that I had been a highly successful computer technician climbing the corporate ladder within the company I worked for and I was happy about it. We were at the beginning of the computer age and yes, I was very angry with myself I let addiction and depression take it away from me and my children's future. I explained that I went to help Jared and our work crews each day after I left my computer job growing our large irrigation business. I told her my pregnancy and additional C-section for my second baby kept me from going right back to work as I wanted to, but it was my mental dependency on the drugs we were doing that was the true problem.

In a much clearer drug-free state of mind and perception in our final session I told her I did not now or ever resent my children in any way. I enjoyed being a mother but I was deeply depressed and distraught discovering my husband had cheated on me so often in our marriage when he was drunk and high. I revealed to her that one night a few weeks back I had returned home from scoring some drugs to find my baby daughter in bed naked with my husband and seeing her crying in distress and looking scared to death was traumatic. I explained the best I could that it was likely that Jared took off a wet diaper, which always made her very uncomfortable and she would wail loudly as soon as it happened, and he passed out before redressing her. I told her the possibility it might not be just what it seemed and the look of terror on my daughter's face when she ran to me I simply could not get out of my mind. I had flashbacks daily after that because of my own molestation as a child and I just could not be certain he had not harmed her in his drunken state. She helped me believe that it probably was just that wet diaper telling me to watch closely in the future how he interacted with my daughter and take immediate action if necessary.

My doctor released me to go home a few days later with a script for Prozac, some breathing and meditation techniques and told me that more exercise and a proper diet would speed my recovery from depression. She suggested I join a group for those suffering from depression and provided me with an extensive list of local groups in our area, and advised me to attend NA or AA meetings. Unfortunately, my limited power and poor understanding of the broader dilemma including Jared's deceptions and misdirection's to the doctors about his own addiction to both drugs and sexual deviancy, and his power to maintain my complete dependency and submission to his control, were not revealed sufficiently because of my fear of him. More so, I did not inform her I had already tried the meeting's approach to recovery, and all these factors combined largely made me even more vulnerable to exploitation by Jared now than before.

I was vaguely aware I must secretively do something to help myself and I asked her on the day I was being discharged if she could recommend some kind of outpatient therapy that might help me. She did and I followed up within a few days of discharge but Jared became suspicious after a few weeks that he was losing control over me and quickly subverted my efforts to alter the path I wanted to take for me and my children. Jared continued to manipulate me and use my children's safety and security as a sword against any effort I made to avoid the temptation of drugs and flee with my children. My fear of almost everything at this point and absolutely no one who I could trust and confide in made me completely vulnerable and helpless short of getting Jared busted and finding a way to support myself and the children. Jared pushed, pulled, and shoved on my fragile emotions and insecurities and used every conceivable falsehood about love and responsibility to guide me back into obedient submission. Those famous lines, 'If you love me', and 'one last time won't get you hooked' – hooked me far worse than ever before and I began a descent into a fiery destructive hell far worse than I could imagine and one I believe no mentally sane person could either> I continued sharing about these previous treatments and relapses with Dr. Pat. Taking them out and retelling the events one by one from my mental music box of hidden tragedies was painful and deeply embarrassing but I prayed every day before the session asking the Lord to get me through them and help me find the answers Dr. Pat said I must have to become well again. Finally, the much sought-after breakthrough happened. He helped me discover through some overwhelmingly horrible sessions during almost four years of running and returning to take another step forward the simple clear answer to the how and why of my addiction. The interwoven rage of the first molestation and so soon thereafter a brutal physical rape by my cousin Pete, the forced secrecy to hide it from everyone forever, and Jared's mirrored repetition and continuance of both dimensions of sexual abuse and forced secrecy to which drugs were added, was the destructive rage in my emotions and my mental responses that fueled my addiction. I had slowly and steadily mentally deteriorated by accepting a false powerlessness quietly and without recourse to produce neurotic submissiveness across almost thirty-five years to accept ending my life and destroying my soul as the only way to stop the pain and suffering that was the whole me.

I had consciously, unconsciously, subconsciously, one or all and maybe more, actively accepted powerlessness to control my own life to the point I truly didn't want to live anymore. It let me go out into the streets for ten long years submitting my body, my mind, and my soul to unspeakable things. I just couldn't outright in a simple act end my own life, or commit suicide at any point. In short, I had experienced too much physical and emotional pain and anguish and had to hide it and together it was beyond what I could endure. The power of the cocaine euphoria was oh so powerful and it deluded me in the most vulnerable times in my life. It deceived me and took away the real power I did have and I let that power slip away... and slip away... and slip away. The power it had let me believe as long as I was high that everything wasn't really that bad... I just had to have enough often enough to solve my problems while I was high and powerful.

Can you see right here and right now what dependency is? Can you see what addiction is? It's a lot of things but certainly doesn't make bad good, pain pleasure, wrong right. The illusion for so many of us is we think the power over the fear, the pain, the wrong, we feel we have while we are high can be held onto or retained when we aren't. It doesn't and wecan't. But is it so ever a powerful illusion that feeds our delusional beliefs, about the next high that will make us powerful or more powerful. On the hamster wheel, we go. Round and round running, running, running. Oh, so sad this first big lie it tells us is and sadder yet is we believe it is the truth.

Maybe none of this applies to you but it sure did apply to me and most of the hundreds I met in recovery. We believed until we were trapped and we ran the hamster wheel for however long we did doing whatever destruction to ourselves and others we did until we didn't. I don't know why or where you stopped believing if you did, or when you stopped running if you have now. But only when you do stop using to flee from whatever truth you are running from or to, do you have any real and lasting power over your own real truth and grab it and hold onto it tightly. I did. I am FREE 'D from my addiction. Along the path to this place I always want to be now, a lot of good people and the Lord helped me discover my real true power and even how to use it.

The best thing I did beyond making the choice not to use illegal drugs that tricked my mind anymore was asking for help. The counselors, the therapists, and the psychiatrists helped me on an adventure of discovery about who I was and who I am, and who I am going to be. They illuminated the darkness and FREE 'D me from self-deception and the deception of others and I overcame debilitating fear, accepted my power, and learned how to be who I needed and wanted to be. It wasn't easy but it was worth doing and I continued to discover how some of it happened and free'd myself from so much shame and doubt.

Indeed much of the pain of childhood I had very little control over and was not sufficiently mentally developed enough to manage it much differently than I did. The same is largely true for my teenage years but maybe I could have found needed help with my issues but not knowing any better I didn't. I simply moved away from home as a young adult thinking I was leaving it all behind and everything would just work its way out. The love and belonging thing set in as it does for most females and I took no active steps to resolve a huge amount of conflict and confusion that was my mental make-up, my own personality. I met Jared soon thereafter and unfortunately, the abuse and repression just continued. I think Dr. Pat was the first to apply labels that I could understand and remember somewhat. A 'Conditioned Response' and maybe another therapist did too earlier and later as well but I don't see myself capable or qualified to use very specific terminology that describes the many complexities of the human mind and how or why we each develop good or not as good as we individually do.

I wasn't really powerless I only thought of myself as being so. Added to this the shame I had steadily internalized and the isolation that was a big part of my life until I was seventeen didn't allow for sufficient socialization and normal development of interpersonal skills and relationships that might have otherwise altered my lonely path. The overarching force in my life was fear and that is so powerful in all of us. Fear is really a good thing to shape our development but at unhealthy levels such as was where I existed, it was so destructive. In my belief system, the balance at the other end of the spectrum of fear is love. And love to is powerful and we need both of them in the right amounts to survive and prosper in our daily lives.

My personal power was regained on that fateful night at the beginning of a long journey that continues to this day and will continue until I ultimately pass away. Each and every day after Dr. Pat sat quietly as I alternated from sobbing hysterically to storming around his office repeating quietly a string of profanities, I understand more about how I deceived myself... repeatedly. Each of us does, and so often we have a lot of people helping us. That is something each of us must discover for ourselves, maybe it's as simple as determining who your enemies were or might be and deciding who your friends need to be.

Making new friends was something I was fearful of as my trust issues had not been fully resolved but I was making progress thanks to Ms. Stella a therapist who had asked me to try a new approach at my therapy. Dealing with the emotional pain with Ms. Stella I began facing the fear of my unknown future and letting go of an unchangeable past.

I understood in a different way than I could have before I became addicted to what the natural feelings and bonding between parent and child were. I can only assume I had them before the cocaine slowly and steadily stole them from me and altered my patterns of behavior so drastically affecting my life and theirs. Ultimately, I relied upon the steady drip, drip, drip of facts and insights provided by those guiding me slowly to full recovery to understand the conflicts for us that were there and would continue to be so in the future. I acknowledged my children had vastly different beliefs about the why of my absences than myself. I slowly learned to feel and understand what their experiences in my absences were and how they would necessarily affect the various aspects of the present and future relationships.

Understanding my absence in their lives as not a choice I made simply to abandon them, by choosing drugs and dark behaviors as more important and valuable than being there with them and being their mother, would not be easy or quick to do. One counselor in particular who helped me see that many conflicts that were there could not be openly spoken by my children was a mother and grandmother herself and was able to reveal to me the confusion they were feeling and might always feel. It would be up to me to undo the conflicts, if they could be undone, by acknowledging them with words and actions that could only over a long period of time change or remove the strong feelings of abandonment and being unloved by me, they each had internalized to various degrees.

The true tragedy that would unfold slowly and complicate the steady change from their belief of being unloved and unwanted by me, to being loved and needed by me even during my absence from their everyday life, was their inability to understand my choice not to be there when they needed me. The counselor was able to slowly and wisely convince me I had to accept for the benefit of each of us, there might always be some degree of suspicion in my children's mind about their value to me. That would, unfortunately, be true to and for others, and the degree of love they could feel and express toward any of us and affect our relationships in negative ways might be permanent. It was hard to accept I might be unable to remove from the mind of my own flesh and blood children that suspicion about my love for them. I might not ever erase the scars of fear and pain they suffered as young and innocent children that forever make them uncertain of how much I cared about them and how deep was my love for them, then and now. It still remains a most painful acceptance all these years later that unspoken doubt might still linger in their minds and there is really nothing I can do to affect it that I do not already do and will continue to.

Ms. Stella opened some other doors of enlightenment that are proving valuable as I continue to connect the dots between my own personal history and its relationship to my children and our future. She touched upon my own feelings from my childhood that could parallel theirs. Not strong abandonment issues, but similar in overall behavioral effect, and similar in that I felt my mother abdicated her responsibility as my mother to protect me from my father's abuse of me. She pointed out, gingerly I guess you would say, that my mother's degree of absence from my childhood home life and relinquishment of tasks a mother would normally do that she made me do instead, deprived me of accurately knowing and affecting as a parent the positive attitudes and boundaries of motherhood. In simplest terms she

EXPLAINED, I could not do within my role as mother to my own children what I did not experience and learn to do within my relationship with my own mother. Lacking any other family relationships from which I could see to learn about motherhood, my knowledge, and effective parenting was going to be limited and that just might be a problem too Ms. Stella asserted.

She told me with professional firmness and human compassion as a mother and grandmother herself, I had to accept the effects my addiction might have had in permanently altering my emotions and my ability to experience the more subtle exchanges that are a normal part of parent-child relationships. She was a little more certain with her professional belief she conveyed to me, the natural maternal instincts of women who have born children that so many say they have inside of them, should not be taken as gospel as always being there so naturally in a woman who has given birth, which meant me too.

She said I should accept that I might not be as maternally inclined as some might say I should have been even without the effects in my brain of the drugs. I understood from her just a little there are lots of subtle but potent words and gestures my children might express that would go unnoticed by me that could lead to misunderstandings and outright confusion. She said that I should even expect them and be prepared to hear more often than I would like from one or both of my children statements like, 'you don't really love me' or 'you don't really care about me,' 'how could you know you weren't even there' and similar doubts and uncertainties they felt.

It was up to me she made me see, that I could not change the factual truth about not being there in my children's lives. However, what I could change was the present and the reality those statements could and would reveal, namely, there might always be a small amount of doubt and I must accept it as being unchangeable, but I must not accept there was nothing I should do to affect it in the future. I should not assure them my absence did not mean that I ever loved them less than I do nor did my absence show I wasn't always concerned about them.

I must she insisted, assure them that the two assumptions or beliefs could not be connected as they were saying they did, that in truth my absence only made stronger my love for them and I was the only one who could confirm what I felt, then or now. I must remove from their thinking that one was necessarily evidence of the other. It took me a little time for what she was offering to make sense, but when the logic of it for them and for me settled in my mind it was clear. The potential differences between adult reasoning and my children's thinking took hold and I followed her guidance and thus far the results are positive.

How do adults change the beliefs of our children? Clearly, it is not as simple as we wished it might be, none the less we don't give up trying when the change needed is a positive one and provides a stable foundation for their growth and maturity. But then again, we first must be right about any change we propose to them for their benefit and simultaneously be prepared to change ourselves. I have discovered or rediscovered, maybe it's a little of both, it usually takes time and great patience to effect changes in emotional beliefs which are not easily identified as such. We all as children and as adults make decisions and choices based on a combination of both logic and emotional thinking. It is a process and for some, it might be more emotional than logical and rational deduction. Clearly, it is never easy or even always productive to ask a child why they think the way they do, or what made them make the choices they did. For me, I have learned that the powers of observation can be the most potent in being a good parent.

Observing and teaching to observe is the easiest way to expand a child's understanding and capacity to think effectively for themselves. We are each unique and in our capacity to experience the environment and the people in our lives varies a great deal beyond just the five senses. I believe and practice to a large degree we are judged more so by what we do, than what we say or believe. I go forward in my relationships with my children especially, and with other adults somewhat, believing that what I do, what others see me do, and how I affect each relationship largely determines the strength and the force of it. What I do for example by having a birthday party at my house for someone, or even the sincere offering of it, goes far in defining the value of the relationship. It is obviously more powerful to show consideration, care, and love than it is to simply say all the niceties about doing so. As the old saying proposes, "seeing is believing," and I believe my children and others whom I love SEE me in their lives now and I sincerely believe it is much more powerful than all the things I might just say and offer up as proof. Thus, I stay engaged with showing the love they all can see if they observe.

I can only advise my children, other family members, and friends about the importance of not bottling up your emotions. Therapy has been instrumental in my complete change in the understanding of the raw, traumatic, emotions and events throughout my lifetime and therapy may be your saving grace as well.

6

Family Affair

The shame many of us feel trying to reestablish our bond with our children is overwhelming at best. Thoughts about how much we love them, how much we wanted to be there for them, and realizing how much we missed are painful when the guilt grips us. Knowing we chose to make our using more important than those we left behind for that elusive high we thought filled us is a painful reality when we feel it. The pain nags at you even more once recovery is chosen like that thorn you just can't dig out of your finger or toe. But it can be dug out and healed in time.

Being back in my children's lives was the best high I felt in a long time. It might actually be the first one with this much new power. It was magical and I thanked the Lord every single night those first few days back in their lives full time. My kids were growing and enjoying my presence again and even though the time was limited it filled me with happiness. It was satisfying contentment I needed to keep going in those early days when I felt the fight really pulling me down.

Letting my mother be any part of my recovery path was a huge problem. It was made harder because she seemed hopeful to see me fail at recovery again so she could feel better about her own place in life. Being the pained, oh so sad, caring mother who for many years went about saving me from my own destruction, or more of it, was the role she wore with pride daily. I wondered if anyone other than me knew what a hypocrite she really was and it angered me to no end that I couldn't tell them for various beneficial reasons a therapist warned. It was a sad truth my therapist helped me discover that the feeling of anger, guilt, and shame she so skillfully imbued me with contributed to the cause and much of the duration of my addiction. It was her identity of great sacrifice before, during, and now even after I have been free of addiction for fifteen years plus, to maintain her hard vigilance to remind me of how much pain I had caused her all of my life in one form or another.

I have never shared with her how much of her domineering personality and her problematic behaviors one particular therapist dissected for my benefit. It was the relief I needed from someone, but most certainly a teacher/therapist I causally befriended through a dating site with impeccable credentials and experience, to further explain why I did some of the things I did as a child and a teenager and illuminate her role in the why and how of it all. I only regret I could never introduce the two of them to confirm some of his assumptions he needed to interact with her to confirm. It remains my secret to this day but the knowledge dramatically improved my relationship with her over the years to the degree it can be improved and it strengthened my resolve to forgive as the Lord says I must.

I didn't let her attitude or actions hold me back or destroy my self-esteem any longer. And honestly, it didn't matter anymore what she thought knowing that it was just better for me to leave behind for good her need for constant attention and praise for all SHE endured giving me birth and being my mother from that day to this.

Her negativity and rejection of me time and again pushed me back to using at a time when just the slightest assurance from her could have made the difference and saved me from almost four more years on the street. All that disappointment, shame, and guilt that I had carried was gone, but the work to achieve it long term was not yet over. Everything of my old life had to be severed, including family who didn't understand me or my addiction or cared to be happy for me or that I was clean and recovering. This could change but recovery rules serve a valuable purpose and I was obeying them vigilantly especially where my over-critical mother was concerned.

I met others in recovery who shared similar problems with family members too. We each need to make the best choice possible about how we will deal with it.

I learned a few weeks after my release while I was at Kurt's that my little brother Mikey was all grown up now so to speak. I was shown a picture of a stocky guy with dark brown hair and brown eyes who lived in upstate Florida with his cute wife and two young kids. He didn't like to be called Mikey anymore and made clear his name was Mike my mother had conveyed. He too, unfortunately, had found his way to Dixie Hwy and the dope boys doing business down there. Mike had become a long-haul truck driver just like our father and it gave him the same freedom to pursue bad choices. Sadly Mike's own painful memories and disappointments in life drew him into the same world I had finally escaped.

It depressed me so much to discover his slow steady path into addiction had started with amphetamines to keep the truck rolling day and night. His wife was so pained and it was hard for her to share just a few facts with me. But I could easily figure out the rest. So maybe I hadn't been just the crazy child, after all, an over-focused teenager, going to work too young, staying away from the brawling Baker house so much I lost my way. Oh my, can a spin ever be put on reality by parents or other relatives when it needs to hide awful facts? I had to wonder just how much of what we shared together, the shame and guilt and the constant and ever so subtle demeaning looks from her that made him too feel worthless.

I did what I could to extract information from my mother and his wife to find a way to contact him. I wanted desperately to reach out to my little brother and explain to him just what that life would bring if he continued on the road he was traveling. Even though he knew via my mother some of what my life the last ten years had been, he didn't know it all and I wanted to stop him from going down as far as I did if I could. I was partly successful and his descent down had not yet gotten to complete destruction of his family, but it was not enough. Addicts, especially highly functional addicts who are highly intelligent as was true with Mike, never believe they have a problem. I was left knowing after our two brief conversations a few months apart all I could do was pray he would escape before the big trap sucked him in completely and he would find his way back to safety soon.

It's normal for families to experience sadness and say things out of fear and hurt. Mine did in the earliest days of our reunion. I understood so very well after therapists had helped me make the necessary connections they had their own special brand of hurt and suffering. There was a need to involve as many as possible of my family who was a part of my life before my addiction and in my recovery journey. I was only partly successful in getting them to go and then to share their perceptions of me and my addiction and importantly their own emotions or reactions. I believed at some point I would be able to get my children into some counseling with or without out me to explore some key issues that needed professional guidance. I even entertained asking them to go to a meeting or meetings with me to get a first-hand look for themselves of what it was about.

I hoped and openly told each of them that one day our new life would shine brighter than the destruction I left behind for them. I wanted them to see I was thankful I had the courage and discipline to fight through so many challenges and be able to show now my determination and dedication to rebuild our relationships. It was what I wanted and what I wanted for them to know was important to me for the rest of our lives. I wanted it for all the right reasons and the primary reason was me because ultimately it is the self that matters first. Before there can be a relationship with another of any kind the self must be ready, willing, and able to be fully capable and honest about desire and ability to commit anything to another. I was ready and I had shown them I was willing because I was right here right now, and I was able because I was committed to never leave them again no matter what. I would let nothing stop me from thinking, acting, and being their mother until I passed away.

Could my children see now the mom that had missed so much of their young lives was eager to be part of their lives now with the desire to share in the joys and struggles of life and watch them grow? Can we each learn or relearn how to love and be loved? Can we share together the ups and downs highs and lows and reshape our world to be what we desired in our hearts? I could only pray it to be so.

I did have doubts and reservations in those first few weeks and months of recovery about all the unknowns and uncertainties of the human heart and love and hate. Will the past just be too much to overcome? Would me and Crystal and Johnnie be able to leave the distresses of the past behind? Are we ready for the pleasure and happiness that could be ahead of us if we were strong enough to reach out and work for forgiving and loving relationships? Needing just a little bit of loving support I called on the Lord in faith to get us there. This was a time of very awkward interactions with my kids as we each learned to be a family. I did my best to show them the love I never received and give love to their children one day. It was my everyday prayer.

I enjoyed my grandchildren and I enjoyed the interaction in their lives more each day. I did the best I possibly could to guide Crystal in these early years of adulthood and I moved to a new place just 4 blocks from where they lived to be able to walk over to be with them. It helped me keep up my physical discipline by walking to their house regularly and I began losing a little of the weight I had put on from all of Kurt's great feasts. Playing with trucks and racecars with the boys or outside on the swing set I shared their happiness having someone to give them a lot of extra attention. It was these wonderfully fun days that gave me the most hope of succeeding in my world filled with all the good things life was supposed to contain.

I remember well the first Halloween we shared together as a memorable adventure for all of us. Crystal proudly dressed the boys up in their costumes one as Spiderman and the other as a Soldier and off we went to collect the treasures in the neighborhood. I took a lot of pictures along the way and it was a night filled with excitement and fun for all, probably one of the most rewarding events thus far on our family journey. They hustled me along anxious to gather as much candy treasure as they could laughing and sharing their little adventure with other kids dressed in spooky costumes we met along the way. I laughed deeply as they ran from house to house reminding them to say, "Trick or Treat" and "thank you," as they collected those sweet treats with avid delight. A bond was slowly forming and growing stronger as the days passed and it was a very secure feeling being in my grandmothers' role.

I was well prepared prior to being reunited with my children that there would be serious issues to overcome. As my treatment and recovery progressed I was helped along by their guidance when unexpected conflicts developed as well. Both of them had a unique perception of the how's and why's of our separation and one by one we opened up the hurt and pain when they wanted to and talked about it. Oh Lord was it painful and full of distress and we had some serious moments that looked like we would not be able to resolve some parts. But slowly they began to accept there was not much if anything we could do about the past but we could do our best to make the future all it could be.

It was a learning process for all because rebuilding trust is not easy, and it is largely what relationships are. I learned from them that I was not the only one having haunting dreams about the past, my children did too and maybe even my mother had them too but she never mentioned that specific reality. I had relapsed so many times and each time made my children less trustful that I would ever be there to be their mom again. I don't blame them because that's what they saw and I died inside just a little each time I relapsed and let what precious trust we had built be thrown away. I can honestly say more of my shame came from that destruction our my relationship with my children and their expectations of me and their trust than all the other horrible things I did to myself or let happen to me. It just traumatized me more and in truth, my consumption of drugs went up proportional to the agony I was feeling most times. It reached a crescendo when Crystal told me never to make her a promise of not going away again when she was twelve years old. I still today feel the pain I experienced when I looked into her eyes that day and saw what I saw. There simply are no words to describe it.

I had told Crystal, "Mommy was going to be ok this time, I promise." She replied with so much anger because she had been so hopeful the many times before and said to me, "Don't you ever make me any more promises, ever again." The tears welled up in my soul that day and it was shortly after that event when I had begun to shift my thinking away from all the shame I thought I could never overcome to the hope that recovery could somehow release me from it if I tried hard enough to get clean just one more time.

I was crushed that day by those words but who could blame a young girl who wanted her mommy there to tuck her in bed every night or kiss that skinned knee after falling off her new bike. I hadn't been there to raise her and what could she believe in the future but more of what she had seen. It was soon after that God intervened once again and off to jail I went. That pain stabbing me deep enough those words repeating often in my mind I knew God was trying to show me the error of my ways and the faulty wiring that needed repair. Praying I would finally make that promise a reality and bring the joy back to my children's lives, I finally made the choice and held onto my resolve that this was indeed the last time I would leave them behind.

My children also saw and witnessed destruction at home with their Father once again. Slowly poisoning himself daily he returned to that same place of drinking and drugging and chasing women. He had gotten off easy when I left all those years back receiving that second DUI with a 5 years sentence of NO alcohol or drugs. That was his choice then at the crossroads in life of his choosing to stay in recovery or move headlong into addiction again. It was up to him to be clean and sober and Jared couldn't choose the right path at all. Unfortunately, Jared thought since he was still successful at feeding, housing, and financially providing for his family that was what mattered. These functioning addicts perceive they are better than the junkie on the street but guess what, they are not.

About the time I was making my first few solid gains in recovery after two months at Kurt's, believing firmly I would make it all work this time as I put my plans into action, Jared started a long downhill slide. I put him up daily in prayers with the Lord every morning and every night hoping he would pull back hard and not fall to the very bottom as I knew he could. He and I had worked so very hard and done so well in building a business before the drugs and his infidelities took me down. Even though we had gone down pretty far before our world together in a marriage collapsed, he held on tight to his hard work can solve everything attitude and fought his way back to the top and made the business again the success it once was and doing several million dollars in business and growing it every year. I had always hoped and I prayed too many a time for his success because the calculated risk I had taken that he would not fail his children was firmly embedded in my mind and I fully believed him more than capable. Though he still indulged in the booze and the drugs and the women after I was gone, it was much less the near full-time occupation he had made it before I left in the middle of the night. He could down a fifth of gin after working all day in the hot sun and do a couple of eight balls of coke himself by 2:00 a.m. and run out of the house at 6:30 a.m. put in a full day working his crews... and repeat, repeat, repeat six days a week. There is no sane explanation for his capacity and endurance that I can imagine, but he did it.

Within a few weeks of my leaving he was faced with some serious reality checks and by the grace of God as I see it, he cut that back to less than half and worked only five days a week to spend time with his kids. After a few months of that, he even managed to go cold turkey on the coke and consumed only a fifth of liquor a week until after another year he got completely sober. He did a good job with his single-parent role with the help of a couple of steady paid girlfriends for a couple of years.

The kids never did without anything, he made sure they went to school and got good grades and heavily rewarded them for doing so. He didn't exactly do it without some serious enforcement and encouragement from the social workers that stopped by making sure everything was going right in the first year or two after our separation. But what really mattered was he got the job done to the degree he did and I am sure there were some really tough days when he was kicking the habits.

I tried desperately to warn him about how addiction will take you back where you left off, how it will drag you under with the speed of a jet taking off the ground just before the tailspin and crash landing happens. Nonetheless, Jared would or could not hear what I was telling him and he didn't want to stay clean and his children watched in horror as history began to repeat once again the year before I got out of jail until shortly after I came out. It's ironic but I think he instinctively knew I wasn't going back down again and I fully made him aware I would be everything in my children's life they would let me be this time. He saw it in my eyes when we talked the first time he met me at the park when I was on furlough to be with them for a few hours. He said as much too after he hung his head when the children couldn't see him and told me unabashedly he had destroyed my life and pushed me into the gutter broken hearted and broken by the drugs. He took all the responsibility he could that day and left with the shame of it hanging around his neck saying he would never forgive himself and neither would God. He only asked me not to destroy him to his children even though he had all but destroyed me in their eyes. I told him he didn't need to worry that he had stayed the course for himself and them and done what he needed to do and nothing, nor I would ever take that from him.

I did all I could every time we had a chance to talk privately assuring him they didn't need to know any more than they did and I wasn't going to hide what I had done from them. I begged him to get clean again for their sake and his own but he shook it off and said he had it under control. I let it go and told him I would just show them the person I really was as their mother before the drugs and stuff, and by showing them me now and build a solid future where we could accept what was done and gone behind us and live in the everyday good that we could make it. I kept my word to Jared and I think he went so far as to take some responsibility for a lot of my own choices to the children. Some of the things I heard them say as we continued to build bridges to the happy future said he had liberated them from some of the lies he had told them over the years. For that, I was deeply grateful to him and I kept reminding them that everyone makes mistakes and their father and I had made our share.

Jared fell into the same fateful trap again when he thought it would be okay, just this one time won't get me hooked again. There will come a time or place similar to this for most of us and we trick ourselves into believing that now that our life stuff is back in working order, or going okay that we can let down our guard and try that fatal: Just this one last time.

Just one last High! One last run at using believing we know how to conquer the beast. If this thought crosses your mind please call someone, go to a meeting, and tell on yourself. Save yourself! Complacency in our recovery cannot take place because it will be our downfall. We must continue to work at it in some fashion daily and even hourly once we have gotten free.

It became a hamster wheel for Jared again unfortunately when the kids saw and understood the abuse Jared gave to his second wife and the hypocritical words he had spoken about me were now showing all too clearly. I was not really at all happy when the horrifying words Jared had said about me were thrown in his face by his son Johnnie. Our son was no longer a little boy running around the yard in his underwear, he was a teenager who had my uncanny power of observation and too well understood that Jared had gotten his second wife Katie hooked on crack and she was pondering that very same thing I had one day long ago. Should I stay or should I go? They had thought they were hiding all their secrets from the children but it became bitterly clear they had just remained mostly silent as long as they could and one day the dam broke.

The same familiar place many partners or family members face along this ugly road of addiction was there again for Jared and he was caught totally unaware. Addicts destroy their home lives as distrust between them grows causing huge fights as justification for lack of money to feed the kids and other nominal things happen when drugs take over and it ripples through the walls. It wasn't money in Jared's house it was the drugs and all the disarray of chasing them and then secretly trying to get high, have crazy sex, thinking kids don't see or hear their strange behavior suddenly begin or blow up in loud fights and things bouncing off walls or worse physical confrontation that distresses and frightens children more than anything imaginable. Katie, Jared's second wife, would have nowhere to go with her own daughter from a first marriage. She didn't work or couldn't due to the drug use. She had just followed along with Jared's manipulative persuasions and left the family and friends she had to stay with him. She was alone with no money and no future and a child to care for if she left Jared.

This is a dire dilemma so many women find themselves in when trying to escape from an abusive life. Jared's destruction of this unassuming woman, who helped raise my kids when they needed someone, was now showing the same issues in every way. The drugs and sexual demands had taken a horrible toll on her and the cost had become beyond her emotional and physical abilities to endure. I almost felt sorry for her and had she not so openly mocked me to my children during the years she had been with them. It was truly a tragedy she was now facing the same reality that had driven me out and away totally a shell of who I had been. I simply had to put it out of my mind hoping somehow her fate would ultimately be better than mine.

As the months swept by my heart was filled with joy attending birthday parties for my grandchildren, the holiday events, or just simply stopping by for a visit to have dinner, all the normal family things that fill the human heart. All those beautiful things we begin taking for granted when we are in our addiction cycle. As your life begins to find that joy in recovery where once you only had sadness you too will be filled with joy as you watch your world unfold sober. Those lonely holidays burrowed away hiding from a life now filled with wonder and imagination is fun when you are a part of the equation.

As things continued downhill for Jared and the delayed reactions from his over-the-hill abuse for more than half his lifetime I could only pray for some miracle intervention and recovery. I had tried to get him to stop, slow down or at least get the much-needed medical help and surgery he desperately required but he only put me off. Watching him turn into a frail skeleton of the man that he once was hurt me deeply even with the knowledge of what he put me thru and what he had done indirectly to Katie and our own children. I now faced the first real close-up and personal death of someone I loved. During recovery, this is something some of us will struggle with, how to undo or bury all the mixed feelings it brings to the surface. All my years of therapy helped me some as I watched his deterioration over the next few weeks. A new and better awareness allowed me to process all those mixed emotions of anger and sadness, love and hate, wondering why he hadn't followed his doctor's instructions. If only he had maybe things would have gotten better. He was the father of my children I kept thinking... just before the thoughts of so much betrayal by what he allowed into our lives illuminated in my mind.

Jared had refused to go forward and conquer life without all the things he thought were making it possible. If there was a simple description that defined who Jared was other than a hard worker, he was more the child who had never grown up. And his problem now was he was 20 years older and had worked in the blazing sun his entire adult life which brought on its own adverse problems. All the coke and alcohol to excess had compromised his immune system too early and skin cancer was eating him from the outside, some kind of digestive cancer in an early stage, and liver cancer on the inside in full force. Jared's self-medicating along with the medications his doctors gave him for pain did not make for a pretty sight at all. Seeing his pain and despair totally crushed my heart the day I went to the hospital to talk with him about what would soon be a reality.

Saddened I could not help Jared because I had to keep going forward, there was no road back to being more than the wife he threw away and consideration for him that he was the father of our children. There was one terribly awkward moment for me. Jared so medicated with God knows what being pumped into his system and knew he was dying but didn't want to be alone in his final days, which he believed would be so much longer than I could see they would be. He wanted another chance with me now that I was a 'good girl' and Katie had slipped away. He said this to me lying in a hospital bed as they were giving him a blood transfusion to try and alter the course his body was following. I left him that day with a warm and true smile that came from the heart of forgiveness God had taught me was the most powerful compassion one could share with another. I forgave him for asking.

A few days later I attended a meeting with a special topic – Death in Recovery. God sure has a funny way of doing that to us. Putting us right where we need to be and once again the message was right on schedule. I know how important going to AA or NA meetings are, I hope you do too. Please listen to that inner voice when it tells you or leads you to do something because most of the time the answer you need will present itself in the strangest of places.

I knew what Jared really wanted and that was for me to join him in his misery. He was looking for something to take away his emotional guilt-stricken pain but I was just not going back down that old ugly road ever again not for him or anyone else. Whether he was delusional from all the meds he was being pumped full of isn't mine to be sure of but forgiveness was the only thing I had in me for him. I tried to give him a hug before I left but angered at my rejection he asked me to leave.

I had completely accepted God was a just God, one who is loving, kind, and merciful; I also knew God was a jealous and vengeful God. This knowledge now comforted me in all my waking moments each day. The world was about to see God's presence in my life. Stronger and more powerful protection and warmth I believed I was earning being a humble and faithful servant to the Lord letting Him choose my life path.

After several solid years into my recovery, I took a brief trip back to Texas to see family and a few friends I had grown up with still living there. No one who had any knowledge about my life after I had left for Florida was ready to believe I had really changed especially my Ma. After all the complaining she had done to anyone who would listen to her tell the story about her worthless daughter who ran out on everyone they all were way tired of hearing it. I think God was too! Because I had changed and I held my head up, carried myself proudly knowing that I could not change anyone except myself.

There was one person that I most wanted to see first, Aunt Hazel. She was the one who always encouraged me and even today reminds me I was always loved. She was the person who acknowledged during that first afternoon, back in my home town sitting with her under a big oak tree sipping tea in an old glider swing with a fuzzy cotton shawl she had knitted twenty-five years ago hanging from her stooped shoulders the good and bad she remembered. She and a few other family and friends had been aware of the turmoil and tumult my home life was growing up. They were mostly powerless she said to affect any change then but held hope my ma would leave that hard-drinking husband of hers and change her own ways too. Her child-raising habits could change then too they believed and she would show care and kindness rather than neglect and animosity before it was too late. They were not so surprised she informed me when they heard the first stories of my distress and the failure of my marriage but they were so certain I had not abandoned my children. They knew me even as a young girl who was always reaching out protectively to my brother and my cousins. It just didn't seem right she said and they each had their thoughts about what happened and what the uncertain future for me and my family was but they prayed always that the Lord would watch over me and them.

Aunt Hazel shared some of my most precious memories of her recounting how she would always sit with me when I was at her place and read stories and watch me play with her cats. I just knew you were going to grow up to be a fine woman one day and it was hard to say goodbye to you when you left but I knew it was for the best she said with a big smile to obscure the little tears I could see in her eyes. Aunt Hazel was indeed the life preserver I clung to during the fearful times and I told her she was the one person who I had missed the most and I was so happy she had lived to see me again in a better way and I was not as awful as Ma might have made her believe. She assured me with a hug when we parted that day she never doubted I would be okay.

She asked about how Ma and I were getting along and I told her mostly the truth. I had spent many years trying to find someplace inside me to put some positive forgiveness and acceptance she simply did the best she could and was not a strong woman or the best mother. I did forgive with a little prompting from the Lord. God said to love your parents so I did but to protect myself as my therapists advised for a good long while, I did not speak with ma except the rare occasions at holidays or her birthday. That was it.

We had spoken briefly over the years and every so often I would call, but I had not been interested in hearing any of the negativity from her. I was also not interested in hearing about any of the family or clan out there in Texas. That part of the world and its mostly bad memories had been left behind me. It was enough to maintain a winning feeling to have conquered the guilt of my childhood and my ma's unloving deeds. I had taken back that last hold on my soul when I shut her out. It did hurt but it truly was for the best for me and that's what was most important now to Me!

Back to God's vengeance and a particular day when ma called me, which was unusual and it caught me off guard. She began telling me about old cousin Pete and how he had died in an accident in his truck. Everyone was devastated back home she said but my mind drifted off to that day out in the barn. It would slowly be revealed that good old cousin Pete was in fact a serial rapist. I could never forget the feeling of his cold calloused hands on my tender skin at eight or twelve and the forcefulness and pain when he pushed his way inside me. My body shivers at the thought. He had unavoidably felt the cold hand of God reach in and snatch his life, probably straight to hell without any discussion about salvation since I don't ever recall that he believed there was a God. He had been out one night driving drunk in that old truck through those back roads in west Texas with another unsuspecting victim riding along. This young pretty girl was barely half his age and had asked Pete a simple question "hey Pete where are we going?" His cold silent look she would later recall scared her bad and she feared something bad was going to happen. Apparently from her recount of events to the police she knew she had to get out of the truck but found there was no door handle on the passenger side door. She did what only a brave soul fearing for their life would do and reached through the open window and released the door from the outside and jumped. Apparently, before he could stop after she bailed out Pete ran off the road and was crushed to death inside the cab when the truck rolled over a few times.

A passing car saw the truck down the little ravine upside down, smoking, and called 911. The police found her curled up in a ball, shaking, crying and terrified when they arrived on the scene.

Her official statement to the police went something like this; "As we got further out on the highway he just seemed to change. He was a nice guy who always talked to me at the football games but he got different when we were riding in the truck. His hand started squeezing on my leg and he wouldn't tell me why we were so far from home. When I realized I couldn't open the door from the inside of the truck, I got scared and reached my hand out the window, opened the door and I jumped."

In the days following the event other girls hearing about Pete's death and the girl, showed up at the police department to tell similar stories of the abuse they too had suffered from the evil that was called 'Pete'. Still, half-listening to Ma tell me this I also hear deep in my soul "Vengeance is mine," says the Lord. "Amen and thank you," I silently replied.

I didn't feel all that good after a few days about Pete's death, but the ugly secret I held in burning me all my life was now made right to some degree and that one very undeserving young girl was spared from an ugly fate worse than scratches bruises and a black eye. But equally important many other girls would never have to fear or suffer at the hand of Pete and hopefully, not at the hand of any of his pals either. I pray for the other boys now men that always hung around with Pete to know there is a God and He might be coming for them at any moment.

Ma's demanding voice brought me back to the present asking, "Tiffy did you hear me? I can't believe that about your cousin. He just seemed like such a helpful good guy when he was hanging around our place. Tiffy, can you hear me?" A thousand feelings rushed through me at the same time, sweet justice most of all, before saying, "Yes ma, I hear you."

Thinking to myself, of course, you don't believe it Ma or you would have never missed what he did to me as a young girl. One day I may tell Ma what happened, but then again why? It was over now and the old saying goes, some things are better left unsaid. Besides, it was now water under the bridge or more precisely, Pete's truck over a little cliff. I was still trying to picture that event in my mind knowing that it was another dark place in my mind and my heart which God had now healed. He had shined His light on it allowing me to move forward with a little more peace and more trust in Him.

Again I hear ma saying, "Tiffany I have more bad news to tell you. Your Pa is dying and I need you to come home soon as you can get here to see him." Oh my God, I thought. Why should I? I knew that alcohol-fueled his rage when I was young and I had taken so many undeserved beatings from him and so had Mike. Yes, Pa had spent time when he wasn't off trucking teaching me to fix and rebuild cars, but seriously there was nothing I wanted to go back home for at all. Too much pain and anger and my therapist had warned me that I might have serious issues if I tried to confront anyone over wrongs they had done to me.

I would rather leave the few good memories and a little

gratitude for teaching me some mechanical skills tucked warmly in my heart than go confront him for his role in a bad show called my childhood. There was just too much to overcome if I went back out there.

The Lord taught me more about obedience as I heard in my mind His words of instruction in the Bible, "Let the dying bury the dead." I understood without a doubt what I must choose and say to Ma, "I'm sorry about Pa being sick, but I can't come out there. With my new job and all that I have going on here it's just not possible." I waited in a long moment of silence for her response and finally said, "Anyways, I spoke to Pa the other day and he told me he was sick. He said he was sorry that I had been forced to leave home when I did and he wished that he had been a better Pa to Mike and me."

I told her after our painful chat Pa and I had prayed together and I blessed him with – Psalms 23.

"I think you were out shopping or something like that when he called," I said.

For whatever twisted reason this made her extremely mad and she went on a long rant at me about my phony shield of Christian salvation to make myself feel better and we have barely spoken since. Fixing the past was not working very well as my kids steadily became more aware of the role their Grandma had played in the life events I endured. I did my best to avoid being harsh and critical of her but she had a nasty habit of saying so many harmful things about me in the worst most degrading ways. I was doing my best to protect them from the more adult aspects of my activities while I was away by telling them a much-sanitized truth about life on the street because they were teenagers and what they heard would bridge a lifetime of perceptions and I left much of the subject matter for a future date with their permission. They accepted my judgment and my feelings that was for the best. Thank my grandmotherly therapist, Ms. Stella, for her mature guidance I followed in handling a very fragile topic for their young minds. As they learned more ugly truths, mostly from her, they invariably were led to them wanting to know from me why or how could she be that way. It was so wrong they said for her to completely reject me at critical times and even more negative feelings for their grandma grew I hoped would not. All I could do was try to soften it a little because it was not my desire to alienate them from her. It is so unfortunate she would do that all on her own.

Ma always believed that she was better than everyone else and was always looking down her nose at everyone who crossed her path, including her own daughter. Ma loved to be around large crowds of people, mostly so she could size them up and see if they measured up to her materialistic reality. I remember her telling me one day that she had so many clothes and shoes that no one would ever see her in the same outfit twice. Why she thought that anyone would care I could never figure out. Sadly ma would finally realize just how a harsh and judgmental attitude during a lifetime had left her with a houseful of stuff and no one to enjoy it with. It made me sad to know it could all be so very different if she would just let the Lord open her heart and her eyes.

It had to happen eventually and Pa died and Ma was crying the day she called to tell me of his passing. I was a little taken back when she asked me what she was going to do now. How would she be able to live? All I could do was listen attentively while remembering those many long conversations we had about planning for this day that she ignored.

I found other ways to soften my kids' perceptions of grandma now that grandpa had died and reduce some abandonment issues more to break this cycle or at least I put a huge dent in it by visiting with my grandkids as often as possible. I searched for ways to be there for my kids forming a family dynamic that had been broken before it was on solid ground. I accepted because I didn't grow up with any positive family dynamic it would be hard to help produce one now without some kind of help *sans* ma and her attitude. When my kids were young and they did speak with their grandma out in Texas all she ever did was talk bad things about their mom and it pushed them further away from wanting to talk to her. For their sake, I had to change this dilemma. I began to read all the books I could to add to the parenting guidance I received in one of the classes in my jail rehab program. It was slowly proving to be one of the best investments of time and effort I had made.

The abuse and neglect I experienced and the broken home stuff my children lived was different only by degree. It was all about trust and emotions. Add to that a few abandonment issues, a little alcohol, the behavioral effect of drugs the kids saw, and presto, you have a complete feast of insecurities and uncertainties that was chicken soup for the mind and the heart! In reality, the mix has a unique synergy of its own that produces a hard to pinpoint and an even harder-to-resolve element of motive. Knowing what in particular motivates a teenager to ask a certain question or make a particular statement or acting out on an issue is incredibly important to effectively navigate the dynamic I was trying to build. For us in the first few years was permanency. Or more simply, was this all going to last? Would we continue to go forward by day, week, month, year without another crash? That was the question I had discovered was always in their minds but rarely spoken out loud. Yes, they did ask a few times in the first year in a cynical way if I was really going to be there on the next birthday or next Christmas, but I had read and believed that question would rear its head in a lot of indirect ways as well. With a flash of insight, and I admit a lot of prayer for a few days on just that point of uncertainty, I adopted the technique of answering their direct question with a question, "Well what do you think today?"

In addressing the question it would only take a little time to probe Crystalor Johnnie on what they were thinking about when they asked the question and ferret out the motive behind it. More frequently than not, it wasn't just abandonment issues not yet resolved fully, it was about how they were PERCEIVING or PLANNING their own individual futures. It would not have ever occurred to me on my own that they were sometimes thinking way beyond an event they wanted me to attend, a birthday they wanted to know I would be at and such, it was how they saw their whole life framed and my role or place in it. Permanence is maybe the most important aspect of healthy maturation in the child-adulthood cycle and it cannot be overstated. Even though it seems counter-intuitive to freedom that you also want a child or young adult to have thinking or choice in, permanence is its base to build on. Think – Choice ... that makes it a little clearer, or at least it did for me.

Given enough time to think critically about how important knowing where you will be living next year, five years, or when you are a senior citizen is more at the forefront of young adult's minds than most parents might believe. If you take this seemingly small aspect for granted or doubt how it applies to our development over the long term, ask a school teacher who hears secrets we as parents don't give much significance to on a regular basis. I learned quickly to add to their security about the future by talking about things I was going to be doing when I retired and lived nearby, or how much I liked living in this city for the rest of my life, or why I didn't want to go some unknown place to live. It was an effective indirect method to cover a broader array of their reasons for asking, or motives if I would be there when they might need or want me than telling them certainly or it's equivalent that was a singular or more temporary response to much bigger mental building blocks they were assembling as their potential futures.

The permanence issue was critical also for their understanding of my physical injuries and my limits including how they might affect my life expectancy. The reality created by injuries I sustained while we were separated did limit me in some of my abilities to engage with them and the grandkids. Without going too deep or specifically how exactly they were sustained, I was open and honest that they were there and the daily effect was not totally predictable. Yes, indeed I had more energy and could run and play in the morning but not so much in the afternoon or evening. I tried to shape our plans together keeping those factors in mind. I made a point of getting as much rest on a Thursday as I could saving up for the weekend frolicking. Weekends were taking them to the local park or down to the beach to play and toss the balls or do a little skimboarding.

There was nothing like a call from Ma on a Monday morning after a great weekend at the beach. Karma has a way of finding you when you least expect it I thought when she tells me my brother Mike is having some trouble. Mike had for reasons only one of my therapists would decipher many years later, believed it necessary to seriously deride and mock me during my addiction. I'm not sure if he thought it might obscure or hide his own escalating addiction I heard about through Jared, or just to be a total jerk. Given how I had defiantly shielded him from so much when we were growing up that he always profusely thanked me for, I was shocked when I discovered, again through Jared, just how far he had gone on some occasions to push me down into the dirt. Nasty name-calling and accusations about what I had done and his own brand of reasons why went well beyond what I would have ever expected from him. I would have called anyone who claimed he did it a liar until he unknowingly did it within earshot of me before I went to jail the last time. But what goes around usually comes around. He now had his own raging addiction ma tells me and he was losing everything he once held near and dear to his heart, his entire loving family.

The following day I received a call from the hospital where Jared was. I had left a request with his head nurse to please let me know first if things started going badly for him because I was the mother of his children and it should be me they heard any more bad news from. She had complied and was making this call because it appeared Jared had refused further life-saving treatments and he was declining rapidly and would likely live only another day or maybe two. I thanked her and said I would let our children and others know.

I immediately called Crystal and Johnnie and as best I could explain their father was not doing too well and it would be best if they could go and see him as soon as they could. They had watched his steady decline during the past year as he lost a hundred pounds and continued without fear drinking and drugging. I made the effort to say a special prayer for their father every time we were together and made it clear that he was doing the best he could to accept his fate. They were at his bedside when he passed away.

Jared was dead four days after his 51st birthday from cirrhosis of the liver and skin cancer, the hundreds of gallons of alcohol, and my best estimate of more than twenty kilos of cocaine. It was a staggering reality but I understood all too well the power and force of that pure white fire to push you beyond any reasonable human limits.

The emotions were raw for a few weeks as I could only watch from a distance, try to comfort them, and pray. It was twelve years since I got clean and just as my healing had taken time, so it would be for the kids now. It was not something they saw coming before it was just there in their face. Jared had hidden his illness from everyone for as long as possible and when he finally told them it was way too late and they never had time to process he was actually ill or worse, terminally ill before he was gone.

These three deaths so close together kind of frightened me. I had every right to wish 'Bad' on all of them but I was never going to roll that stone back on myself by asking God to take them from this world. His justice had prevailed and even though I want everyone to be good and live a long life by nature, I could only trust that it was Gods doing to help me heal. They each were monsters in their own unique way and they had done me great undeserved harm, and I could not repress the relief I felt for a time. I could not because every prayer I prayed about the feeling of release and calm I was experiencing God simply made clear that I wasn't bad for feeling it and He did it until I stopped asking about it daily two months later. He or maybe it was their passing or both gave me a sense of security I had never felt before. Peace and acceptance like the prayer say, are pieces of the puzzle that gives you serenity and that's what I was feeling.

I was now a successful, socially acceptable, tax-paying, law-abiding citizen and I was proud of myself. Step by disciplined step I had earned the respect I was receiving from myself and people who knew me and it felt amazing. I felt something entirely different than I did the night I was shivering in the cold on the jailhouse steps wondering what the future had in store for me. In my mind, I saw myself lying on the sandy beach on my favorite blanket with the sun warming me listening to the waves roll in and out and the birds screeching happily above while pondering what the future had in store for me. Faith, obedience, discipline, hard work, and prayers can do a lot to transcend you in time.

Pondering the future I see that it is finally time for me to enjoy all the hard work I have put into rebuilding my life. It was time for some gifts to be given to me, simple things I had found were the very best gifts of all. So I created a new list from the one I had managed to cross off and successfully completed all the initial goals from so many years back. It was time for some new plans and fun!

The most precious Gift indeed, is Today, as no one is promised a tomorrow.

So I had been practicing what I preached and enjoyed this day and I reminded myself before I smiled and said; "Lord thank you for watching over me, my family, and for bringing Gideon as a new friend and protector into my life. Someone who knows your words from the good book, someone to explain the Bible to me and your teachings, ones that even after twelve years of study I still want more understanding. Someone to help me understand what is my purpose that you have given me in this new life. How do I go forward to prevent others from traveling down that same ugly road, a lonely, painful road filled with destruction of unimaginable proportions?

My family affair now and into the foreseeable future is pretty much like most families in America and to a large degree the world over. I have made myself into the mother I always wanted to be and the grandmother too and I hope I can stay healthy and live long enough to call out the name or names of my great-grandchildren. I have made just a little progress with my Ma but she is still a stubborn one hanging out too much in the past or reciting all the problems of the present rather than enjoying the good in each day she has remaining in her life.

My children's lives have followed a fairly predictable life path thus far just like so many others who are the product of broken homes and drugs. And just like others Crystal and Johnnie each reacted differently to the same set of circumstances. I understand the fundamentals of males and females having entirely different responses, one emotional more so than the other and one physical more so than the other. For females, the social norms against aggression are pretty straight forward but boys are almost expected to be aggressive or highly competitive and display violence to some degree as just being boys. Johnnie had a few more fights with boys usually bigger than him than he should have and has a few small scars to show he wasn't always the winner. But largely being he acted to protect others physically or shield a female against unfair accusations, the 'acting out' of emotional issues... his fights and scars are medals of valor in my mind. Do you have to wonder at all what that common high school bad boy's assertion about a female's sexual promiscuity might have been?

In light of what his Father's completely unthinking and destructive description of his mothers' activities surely was when he was high and intoxicated, it is very easy to see how hyper-reactive Johnnie would be when hearing a female classmate being degraded with that accusation leveled at her regardless the merit or the size of the accuser. I readily see how some of his insecurities or emotional conflicts got worked out. Only recently was my little Johnnie, now a sure and confident adult with very high standards, able to even speak to his mother about those very ugly words he heard in reference to me and other females he knew. I saw in him a very endearing kind of nurturing protectiveness that can only come from a man who has worked out for himself some very complex dilemmas about what character is and what integrity means. His wife openly asserts it is what attracted her to him and it's who he is inside and out. He likely didn't learn much of it from his Father thus leaving me to assume behind that quiet demeanor he projects is a mind, or is it perhaps his soul, fully engaged in being a man Jesus would likely approve of.

Crystal indeed had some early issues with passive-aggressiveness that one of my counselors stated is a normal response to insecurities related to abandonment. Even though Jared usually had one or more females around, they could not likely or easily form the trusting natural bond Crystal needed to navigate some sensitive strictly female realities. There are things that a young healthy maturing female can't easily share with someone other than an attentive biological mother that is critically important to her teenager-adulthood maturation. Therein were created uncertainties that plagued her well into her adulthood and her role as wife and mother. Understanding her sexuality and all that this entails as a teenager and then a wife weren't effectively dealt with nor were the more important realities of emotional needs and what a relationship with a man or a husband was about.

Crystal ultimately married too early, had too many babies too soon, and unhappily divorced the father of her children having clearly picked a boy that didn't mature for whatever reasons and become a strong stable husband or the best full-time father. I was not asked about her choice of a husband or the relationship she needed. She decided she was going to get married and did and I accepted my limitations. The young man she chose, or maybe was it she let him choose her, did bear some significant similarities to her father and I liked him when I first met him. He was tall muscular and handsome, showed her lots of affection and attention, and showered her with gifts for a time, but he ultimately didn't stay the course and become the hard-working devoted family man Jared was her model for. Even given no one woman was ever enough for Jared and until the last few years of his life Jared heavily guarded his drinking and drugging from her and Johnnie, Jared projected an honest image of strength and self-security and devoted fatherhood that isn't easy to match and drugs didn't deter him from being. Slowly she let me into her comfort zone and we were able to untangle her emotions from rational decision making and illuminate what the future should be if she uses her head instead of her tender emotional heart and insecurities as a woman that let her down hard. We are crossing into new and challenging areas for her that she has to learn to navigate better. Being a single mom now and all the myriad problems associated with rejoining the workforce full-time instead of part-time, caring for her children with only limited participation by her ex-husband, cooking, cleaning, and doing the laundry and, well, sleep might become something of a luxury!

She has high expectations for herself now and I can only hope and pray together we share in making better choices for her future than she did trying to do it all on her own, or worse falling into some rebound relationship with a man less than what is ultimately required. If I can teach her the power of a steady disciplined approach to a seemingly, and honestly sometimes it is as well, overwhelming task of becoming Superwoman with reasonable expectations, we can all be winners! Setting the time every morning or every night with pencil, paper, calendar, and determination to establish some realistic goals is good work that needs to be done. Mapping out the series of little steps up the big mountain she has to climb, will reduce a long hard marathon climb into a steady hike on flat ground the paper plan can make it into, revealing her inner strengths with a little help from the Lord and a willingness to see it being successfully achieved in her naturally willful passive-aggressive mind first. That's my take on the old axiom 'Seeing is Believing.'

Johnnie, well not many surprises there really so far, and not much I need to help him and his wife with anymore but happily babysitting my grandchildren. He was always quiet anyway and his highly competitive personality and his father's willingness to let him tag along with him as he grew up allowed him opportunities Crystal didn't have in the same way. Being out in the field with his dad after school, Saturday, or full time in the summers with a shovel in his hand or operating equipment gave him plenty of exercise, and having his hard-working Father as a role model made a boy into a serious, self-assured, comfortable in his own skin, Alpha male. At eighteen years old he was supervising large work crews who respected him not as the boss's son, but as a hard-working foreman who led by example, much like his Father.

He quietly honed his business skills at night year in and year out at a plan table or behind a computer screen bringing together men and equipment to manage million-dollar jobs at twenty-one. When Jared passed away Johnnie stepped up and managed the business for a year before selling it to investors and employees deciding he did not want to follow his Father's career path any further. He chose another construction career and after another year of school as an Ironworker, he is a foreman on large-scale industrial projects throughout Florida. He met a sweet girl, gave me some more grandkids, bought a new home, hardly touches a beer, and is a youth pastor at their church.

Crystal gave me three wonderful grandchildren to enjoy and Johnnie has given me two, the youngest adorable little girl is almost three months old today. Some days I feel like I never missed a day in their lives, and judging by what they sometimes say with a smile and a big warm hug, they feel the same way. Maybe God's hand and words of assurance were there with them in my absence, which even that too they say is true more often now than in the first years on this journey with us all together. When their fears were gone and they felt certain they shared the very words of the prayer requests they gave God to fill, and I came home to them for good. There is no feeling I know greater than that given from a child, be they young or old when they say 'I love you, Mom.' It fills a cup that nourishes the heart and the soul and from that same cup you give them the 'I love you too' they need to grow and prosper. Love merges unto itself from two points in the universe and for those of us who know God sanctifies it and magnifies it with His own love that which He created to be loved. Each day is its own unique story and it has a beginning and an end. In between the sunrise and the sunset of each day is part of an important journey which we close with rest and reflection of where we started and where we are now as darkness closes in once again. I no longer fear laying my head down on the pillow and closing my eyes frightened by what is ahead in my dreams, fearing for my life or fearing for my children's, or trying to push away the thoughts of what I had just done or what I must do tomorrow. Gone is the sadness and despair, disgust and shame, and the inevitable hopelessness that will come seeing no escape from the trap that held me in the darkness that I had once become. Free 'D, I am, and I am content and the darkness that surrounds me now each night as my head rests on the pillow is time to pray and give thanks to God for all He has done in this day of my life. It was all good and I was glad I lived it with all of its challenges and all of its joy. I can reflect on my children's happiness for all that I have done and all they have given me. Love and hope, wish and fulfillment, give and take, ask and receive, it was all there today.

I can rest my mind tonight and await the dreams and messages that transcend time and all the boundaries that I can see. As I let it all in and give it all up, the silence reveals a presence and illuminates my way to give to others of that which was given to me. My vision is clear and I am sure the journey of this day is now absolute and my will to follow, let go and release my prayers fulfilled this day is complete and now I sleep.

I am what most describe as a highly disciplined person. Part by choice and a large part necessity in recovery I set pretty specific large goals and key objectives for myself and loosely mapped out on paper a plan for accomplishing them. As time went by I expanded a dozen or so pages of my recovery plan requirements into a highly refined and detailed life plan. Hours, days, weeks out into a year of goals and activities to direct my life. With a calendar handy I jot down some keywords, some kind of time aspects, and then go about refining the objectives into a daily planner. It's a simple thick-lined spiral notebook that translates the data from little scrap paper worksheets into specific names, dates, times, and places onto a schedule for a year. It solves trying to remember everything or keep track of too many sticky notes that used to accumulate everywhere into a single guidebook that can fit nicely into a pocketbook that can go anywhere. For simplicity, it keeps me attuned to responsibilities and commitments and just seems to make life much simpler to direct and manage.

There are a few more little snippets of my family affair contained on the last five pages in a couple of those notebooks that are significant to where I am today and how I got here. Equally important are the notes I made about starting an outreach to others like myself that struggled with addiction and recovery and all points in between. Everyone, addict or not, has in their lives some turning points, crossroads, significant events, or people that majorly affected their life. If you were an addict maybe you remember the day you first got high or who influenced you to make that bad choice. If you are recovering, remembering the day you got clean if you are. Those days are significant and every day thereafter is too. One particular morning while scanning through one of the old day planners sitting in my favorite place to say my prayers and reflect on the day ahead or the days behind sometimes, I returned to the fateful day my soulmate Gideon and I first met. It is the last piece of the family affair that we have shared thus far. Crystal had told me of the Christian charity and the pastor who was in charge of a house her husband had found to rent they wanted badly to move into. They desperately needed a bigger and safer place to live than they were in at the time and she described it to me and it certainly was what they needed. I got one of those tingling sensations across my scalp while she was telling me about it that I knew was oh so special. I instantly felt

God working in my life once again right then at the moment. She asked if I wanted to go over and see it with her a little later in the day. I told her of course I did and she said she would be back after she ran some errand and we would ride over there.

We arrived in the neighborhood in a nice part of town and drove into a residential neighborhood with nice-sized houses with trees and manicured lawns. My first thought was what can they afford in this neighborhood? We pulled into the double driveway of a pretty gray house with white trim and a big two-car garage.

"Is this the house?" I asked Crystal. I could hardly see them moving from the little place they were in that they could almost afford to something this big that had to be three times the rent. "Yes, it is. Isn't it nice? Wait till you see the backyard, its just huge and there is a swing set. And the inside is beautiful and it's huge too. I hope we can get it," she smiled answering excitedly.

"Well I hope you do too but just how are y'all planning on paying the rent on it? Did Terry get a new job to pay for it?" I asked thinking without some big change in what they were doing I just couldn't see it happening. But I did hope that it was true because it would be an answer to my prayers for certain.

We looked around the house and at the big backyard and peeked through the windows and indeed it was a great place for them to live. We finished our little tour and put the kids back into the car and Crystal drove me home.

"I will be praying for you, Crystal. I hope it all works out and you can get it and make some progress you need in finding a job. Looks to me like you will need more than just Terry's salary to afford living there. That's a really big house and rents can't be cheap in that neighborhood," I told her.

Indeed a few days later she called me very excited and practically screaming that they had got the house and were going to move in a few days. She asked if I could help them move and I told her I would and asked when did she want to get started packing? I was startled by her answer, "Tonight! We have to be out tomorrow or else they will lock us out if we don't pay more rent here for another month."

All I could say was okay but I couldn't come over till in the morning it was just too late tonight but I would be there at seven and do what I could.

We got them all packed up and got everything in the U-Haul truck with the help of all the neighbors she could enlist to help us. I followed them over to the new house on Cumberland Drive and we started unloading the truck. When I walked through the front door with the first box in hand I was a little surprised when a well-dressed gentleman with a warm smile on his face came out from one of the bedrooms and said, "Hi, let me help you with that box please." My mind instantly told me this man was everything Crystal had conveyed to me about him. I felt something exactly as I did being greeted by the minister at the church I was attending. He kind of exuded a sense of warmth and integrity that you would instantly feel comfortable with.

It was as if I had known him for a long time and we were seeing each other again after a long separation. We both had just kind of frozen in place, me standing there with a box full of dishes and Gideon standing there just smiling with his arms extended to take the box from me. There was something special about him, warmth radiated from him, like an old soul shining a bright light in a dark place. A bond formed between us before another word was spoken and I knew my prayers were answered for me to have a friend and someone to give me strength. Neither one of us could unlock what we were feeling as we stood there just holding each other's eyes with a steady gaze. It was just a strong sense of connectedness that I had never felt and I was sure in my mind in that long timeless moment it was, he was feeling something strangely familiar too.

"Please," he said, "let me have the box and tell me where you want it to go."

His words broke our gaze and the daze I was in and I let him take the box from me. "Well, I think it goes in the kitchen. Just put it on the counter for now and we can put them away later," I said and turned and went out to continue unloading the truck.

There was much I wanted to know about Gideon. This man who came out of nowhere and connected with my soul was someone from my past that I had forgotten... or someone in my future capable of opening my heart again.

7

Transcendental Meditation

Building beneficial and stable relationships after my recovery journey began when I stepped out of jail for the last time was a slow and challenging process. A little more than six months clean and only a few weeks at Kurt's adjusting to my freedom, I had made critical choices about using my time and efforts to make friends beyond Kurt. The only thing of certainty was attending NA meetings and I was determined not to repeat mistakes of the past initiating the wrong kind of friendships with people who could upset the fragile stability I had at Kurt's. The first few meetings I attended I made no efforts to go beyond the normal introductions and casual discussion about how long I had been clean and the tip of the iceberg discussion of my addiction experiences. Slowly I opened up a little and by the time I had attended a dozen twice-weekly meetings, I was exchanging phone numbers with a few females and was being more friendly but reserved in exchanges with a couple of non-threatening males at different rooms.

There were some surprises along the way learning about people just like myself in the rooms who for one reason or another had gotten too close to the fire and got consumed by it. Casual use of alcohol or marijuana was fine I often heard and for most was the common thread until the fire got too hot and casual use became every day or sometimes even all day everyday use and that's called abuse. I knew that story all too well and after a year of meetings, I didn't have a problem opening up about some of the dark roads my addiction had taken me down. Not all the roads by any means, but many of the things I needed to let go of, discover or share and learn from others as I walked the twelve steps to freedom one step at a time. I had taken a couple of the steps more than once before because I relapsed a time or two but finally I got right. Meeting after meeting close to home and a few times far out into another county to AA, NA, OEA, and others I went sharing a little bit of me but listening more to the experiences of others trying to understand if I was unique or were we all the same? Often I would just pray and ask my higher power, which was the designation for that force or entity that was greater than you and could help you find your way out of the darkness if I should try another room and I would run my finger down the three-page list for my general area until something said this one and off I went to hear and be heard.

Tying to avoid the temptation of Friday night parties or clubs where drugs and alcohol of every description can be hard to reject, a meeting was the safest place to avoid an easy road to relapse for most of us in the early stages of recovery. It was Friday and I was out late in the afternoon to do a little window shopping and pick up food for my birds. I got back into the car after making the purchases at the pet store and pondered for a few moments what to do with what was left of the day and night. My Friday night routine on a bad day was a smokey room meeting somewhere close to home if I was feeling anxious or overstressed and didn't have any kind of engagement with family or friends. The alternative on an okay day was a little ice cream while reading a book or lying on the couch watching TV until sleep overtook me. Neither seemed to be right for tonight so I closed my eyes, took a slow deep breath expecting I would simply obey a simple heads or tails mental coin flip. Or maybe I should take the time to be still for a few moments longer and pray about it. Well...

The Fisherman's Net Church came to mind and was only a few miles from where I was. The regular meeting time there was 6:30 p.m. so I decided to just head over there a little early and perhaps be the first one to arrive rather than going home and then back out again to attend the 7:00 p.m. meeting of regulars I knew much closer to home. I had gone to meetings at the 'Net' twice during the early part of the previous year and both times the mixed group of guys and gals were mostly younger than me. Only one, a tall stout friendly gentleman ex-biker a little older than me I met at my first visit there, was recovering from long-term addiction. Maybe he would still be going there. He was an amphetamine and cocaine user for seventeen years and stated he was almost two years clean to the group who had an average addiction period of about three years and were all in their first year of being straight.

Like most other meetings I had gone to on a Friday night I expected to see the usual five to eight regulars. I was a little bit confused opening the door to the designated room and seeing well more than a dozen people milling around inside standing in a couple of small groups and talking. My first thought peering through the door was they were not a recovery group meeting and I was probably interrupting something to do with the church that was preceding the meeting in the room. I was closing the door quietly when I heard Arnold, "Arnie," the Florida native who befriended me during my first visit here, call out my name and I saw him with a hearty grin waving for me to come on in. Shy me was a bit relieved and I went in and walked over to Arnie and exchanged hellos and glad to see you again or happy to meet you as he introduced me to everyone there. A few of them I remembered from previous meetings and those I did not already know were a friendly and varied group of old and young male and female and diverse but balanced ethnicity. After the round of introductions, Arnie asked if I was ready for a cup of coffee and I said yes that would be nice. He walked us over to the well-provisioned long tables set up in a back corner of the room where four shiny silver tankards labeled REG or DECAF were sitting. I was just a little surprised by the variety and amount of food and snacks arrayed on two six-foot tables and three large cooler chests sitting beneath them.

I quipped to him with a big grin as he handed me a Styrofoam cup for the coffee, "It looks like you are having a big banquet for somebody tonight... or have you converted a whole bunch of ex-addicts into health food junkies with big appetites!

He returned my humor with a big grin and said, "True on both counts little lady. Tiffany since you were here last we gained a few souls and got a couple of sponsors and one is actually beating back the demon and doesn't miss many meetings either. He runs a catering business and of course, he told us that was how he got addicted both times, setting out spreads and drink bars out on the island for a couple of big-time dealers of our former favorite delight. A time or two he didn't indulge himself in the beginning cause it was all about business. But you know the truth it is for sure, you stand too close to the fire long enough and you gonna get burnt sooner or later, right?"

I nodded affirmatively reflecting for a long hard moment about how true that was for me. We sipped the coffee and exchanged brief histories about what we had been doing since we had last seen each other. His cell phone rang and he excused himself to take the call and said he would be right back and stepped away. My thoughts returned to his comments about too close to the fire and how I had allowed addiction to really take hold of me only when I went back with Jared after my second try at rehab. I almost broke free from the big trap. But I was so damn naïve to believe I could stay straight knowing full well that Jared wouldn't stop drinking and drugging and all that went with it just because he promised me he would. But I was young and scared, still full of the hopeful storybook and TV illusions, and thought I could stay straight even if he didn't... and paid the highest price for standing too close to the fire.

Arnie reappeared and said, "Hey," it jarred me back into the present and I followed his gaze toward the entry door as a middle-aged couple and a half dozen more people came through the door, "guess we can get the show underway now Tiffany, our fearless leader has finally arrived. Let's go introduce you to Paul and his group." I quickly set the half-finished cup of coffee on the back corner of the table closest to me and moved in beside him to meet and greet the newest arrivals.

A casually dressed well-groomed man I guessed as mid-forties, and a slightly younger-looking woman I assumed was his wife or girlfriend in a long flowery sundress, was accompanied by four others who appeared to be couples as well. With smiles and extended hands, Arnie and Paul alternately introduced me to each of them. Indeed Paul, the fearless leader I presumed, was accompanied by his wife Rebecca, Raoul's wife was Louise, and Marcus's fiancée was Shauna. Arnie excused us from the group after the lengthy round of introductions and small talk and explained as he led us to our seats in the second of the six rows of chairs that had been set up while we were chatting and meeting the new group that Paul and Shauna were going to be the main event tonight. Arnie beamed broadly as he related how he had been the person who was instrumental in getting Paul to move and bring his growing group of followers from the small and stuffy, overcrowded room used for babysitting Sunday school toddlers at a Presbyterian church at the other end of town. He leaned in close after we had taken our seats and said in a conspiratorial whisper, "Raoul is the caterer I told you about and this big room we got here is plenty big enough for him to share the abundance with us leftover from his customer's big parties. And no, he doesn't do the hot shindigs for the dealers no more, but he does lots of business with plenty of the Wall Street types and their friends out on the island. No... they ain't junk food eaters either and we ain't too prideful of accepting their leftovers none whatsoever."

His hearty low throated chuckle made me feel even more at ease in this large room of mostly strangers. But I was startled when I felt that hard rippling tingle in the top of my brain that occurred only a few times in my life when I was in very deep meditative prayer. I simultaneously saw a fleeting mental image of how it was that I was here tonight instead of sitting in front of the TV accepting a little loneliness was a necessary part of my recovery. The Holy Spirit had guided me here from the pet store when I was conflicted about my choices and vaguely mumbled silently... Lord help me... with not a lot of expectancy at that moment on such short notice to Him.

Paul had walked up to the front of the room and was standing there and I guess was about to say something when one, then two, three, and then everyone in the room was clapping serious applause, and Arnie and I joined in. I glanced briefly at Arnie wondering if I had missed something and he was nodding his head up and down with a wide smile and shouted out into the din of noise. Let's hear the Master speak fearless leader!

The applause slowly subsided only after Paul had raised his arms out like wings and gave the familiar up and down motions to bring it down or stop. His face got a little pinkish, he was clearly blushing, and I was close enough to see the twinkling look in his eyes that was usually a prelude to tears. This was certainly like no meeting I had ever been to and whatever was the signal or the cause for which the applause had started was indeed significant to most or all present. I didn't see a tear appear as clapping and conversations ceased and quiet returned to the room. Paul reached into a pocket and pulled out a cell phone, held it up and pointed at it with his free hand, and said, "Okay we know the rules. Phones silenced guys and gals."

I was startled by the sudden phone alert noise emitted by the cell phone Paul was holding up. He too appeared startled judging by the pained look on his face that said no, no, not now please, shaking his head staring at the phone. He turned his attention back to us, grinned broadly, and said, "Oh well... we can get started in a couple of minutes, I got to take this sponsor call." Quite a few people, myself included, laughed knowingly at his visible dismay as he walked briskly from the front of the room and out the door. I wondered if it was really just a humorous gambit and part of the act I was expecting him to engage us with and if anyone else was thinking the same.

I had set my phone to vibrate before I had gotten out of the car but I reached into my pocket and double-checked anyway. The four people in our row sitting to my right mostly did the same and started conversing about similar events happening to them and I surmised they didn't think the phone call was any kind of a gambit. A few subdued conversations and exchanges had begun in the room and I nudged Arnie when he appeared to have finished talking to Marcus, the soft-spoken black gentleman who was Shauna's soon-to-be husband, sitting to his left. "Is Paul a comedian?" I asked.

Oh no," I said, "I thought you said he and Shauna were the main event tonight and the clapping and the phone made me think a routine had started."

"Oh, oh, oh, right! You haven't been here and we didn't get to finish our conversation about what all we have been doing here at The Net. I don't know how much time we got before Paul gets back, I'm sure it won't be long, but listen here."

"I was going to a little church on Fairway Drive out by where I moved to when I first got straight. Sandy Cove Christian Church, little place, couldn't hold but thirty-forty people max, built back in the early sixties when Sandy Cove wasn't more than a thousand acres of swampland and a little ole bait store, gas station... you wouldn't believe that now would you? Anyway, developers came in and drained some of it and subdivided it on paper, and sold building lots to the Yankees up north over the phone. To make it seem like a more legitimate place to want to buy land to build a house in Florida, they built a little wood-frame building on a high and dry spot, painted it white and put a big cross on top, and called it a church. Had nothing but a tiny little sand parking lot that couldn't hold more than ten or twelve cars at most. Sandy Cove Church was really just an empty shell of a building but it looked good blew up big in the fancy sales brochures they sent up north all those years. Anyway, the original land developer was going to tear it down when the city took everything over to incorporate it all in 1997. A local fellow named Alton Jessup, Paul's daddy, who actually helped build it when he was a teenager working construction, persuaded them to sell it to him cheap for a real church. Alton, who was a Gideon, you know the ones that used to put the Bibles in the hotels and hospitals, well he put some old wooden pews and a piano in it, and got a retired Pentecostal minister to come and preach to his family and friends on Sundays. So it was Sandy Cove Pentecostal Church for a while. I went there one Sunday morning the first time I tried to get right because it was walking distance from my house and there wasn't but a couple of cars in the parking lot and I figured an old broke down, bike ridin' drug bum like me wouldn't get mugged badly by a mob."

I couldn't suppress laughing at the images his southern drawl and wordplay painted in my head. Big old biker Arnie in full colors and chains astride his Harley fleeing from the church parking lot in a cloud of dust as finger-pointing bonneted Pentecostal grandmothers shouted at him to repent from his errant ways. I just couldn't stop laughing as tears came and Arnie was laughing too and I was thankful the Lord guided me here to meet a new old soul.

It had gotten quiet and mine and Arnie's fading laughter almost prevented us from noticing Paul had returned and was almost back to his center-stage position and we froze into silence. I knew there was much left to know about a little white church and Arnie and Paul's journeys that brought them and their friends to The Fisherman's Net, but I guess it would have to wait. Paul was front and center... holding a big red Bible in his hand. A shiver ran through me and a new dimension of calm assuring feelings of trust and understanding unfolded into where I was and who all these strangers were and why we were here made perfect sense. Indeed, Paul looked like he shouldn't be anywhere else and I believed neither should I.

Paul was looking out at us with a soft smile and slowly nodding his head with an approving gesture gazing back and forth across the rows of people that were his rapt audience. When his eyes met mine he paused for a long moment and I felt a tightening in my gut thinking he was going to acknowledge me in some way or say something to me or about me. But he didn't and he continued to scan his audience and I instinctively knew then he was connecting with each person individually and perhaps I might be the only first-timer present tonight and he had given that extra heartbeat of time acknowledging a new relationship between us.

"It's good to be here again with you and I am glad each of you came here tonight too. And honestly, I wish I knew what or who the applause was for because I think I must have missed something," he said looking around behind him and up and over his head in a mock gesture of curious bemusement.

"Really... What's the occasion?" he continued with mock inquisitive sincerity. A burst of subdued laughter rippled through the rows. Nice. I wondered where this was going to go because it certainly was not the way AA or NA meetings started I had ever been to. Where would this meeting leave me feeling when it was over I wondered.

Recovery isn't something that makes you all smiles and happy-go-lucky, life is but a dream, amusing kind of thing. No, not at all. Addicts and ex-addicts, at least any I had ever been around on and off the street after a short period being clean were normally somewhat tense, maybe jittery too, and wary of being close up or overly friendly unless they were making a play for something or scoring drugs. Acting or at least pretending all was cool and they had not a worry in the world. Faking it to make it. Unless you were high and happy at the moment and were someplace you believed you were safe, being friendly and open was not the attitude except for those well along in recovery that had conquered all or most of the addiction-recovery demons. They were kind of few and far between in smoky rooms unless they were the Chairperson.

Scared and uncertain, tired and weary, that just wasn't here in the room tonight. No one except maybe Paul and one or two of the others I had met tonight didn't openly show at least some signs illuminating who they had been and why they were here. Too thin, or nervous and fidgety but trying to hide it, or a little awkward exchanging greetings, or long sleeves when it was summer, hot and humid outside this room, the signs were all there, they each had been trapped and recovery was still a one day at a time process. But still, there was something decidedly different about this group and this meeting and it wasn't just familiarity with each other that made it so different. There was trust... and that was hard to find anywhere, for the addict or non-addict alike.

Unfortunately, the modern world we live in thrives and prospers on deception from which mistrust is the natural result for all of us. From the most simple and overused going out of business sale, or last and final chance, or only one left at this price ploys, through the steady growth of misrepresentation and outright lies thrown at us in every form of media, deception is everywhere all the time. Without our consent or approval, we are constantly pushed, pulled, and sometimes forced to believe the impossible, accept the unreal, deny visible reality, and suspend our own natural valid judgment. Thus mistrust in most anything is a necessary part of survival. And so we all do... or is it we don't? Either way this real and expanding paradigm of mistrust drives most all of us further apart and the imbalance between people in the natural cooperation toward progress grows. The reinforced imbalance increases the mistrust and chasm between the haves and have not's. Productive human relations and the natural development of interpersonal skills and relationships continue to decline between parent and child, teacher and student, husband and wife, and we are all worse off for it each and every single day. It extends fully into the dominion of man and his Higher Power, and the relationship between man and his loving God. The irony is... who wouldn't want to do mind-altering drugs at least once amid the chaos of reality destruction? Further still, who can we trust to guide our recovery to 'safety' if we choose to return to the deception in the world... and fight back?

It had been mere seconds since Paul's humorous question about the occasion for applause. Within my own mind and soul, decades of thoughts and experiences were illuminated in a single intertwined reflection of challenges and dilemmas about trust. The occasion here and now for me was I felt good and I was okay being with all these strange people I really didn't know and I was glad I was here and I trusted completely it would be a better – 'stay clean meeting' – than many I had been in on my recovery road.

What Paul did next was converted me. I believe everyone in the meeting with me that night who might have already begun their journey with him, learned to transcend beyond our unnatural dependence on deception and mistrust in the world and advance ourselves. He united all present tightly and formed a strong bond between us beyond our common truth of having once been addicted and now bonded us in recovery... together. He taught us, and we learned how to attain the next level of human awareness and personal development. We were FREE 'D from our addiction beliefs and FREE 'D from the debilitating negative stigma 'drug addict' made us and we allowed others to reinforce, and by our own choice, we were FREE'D from 'being alone' without a higher power or God, and FREE 'D to be... anything we chose to be.

"We are the occasion," he said with warm and directed emphasis and scanned each row, and paused long enough at each person one by one to nod and show he was talking to each of us and not at us. "We have two new souls joining with us on our journey tonight and I hope Tiffany and Allan will both find comfort and enjoy being with us as we share ourselves with you and you share yourself with us. Our journey to our freedom and well-being only grows with your presence as we grow together and find strength in our unity. Our purpose as fellow travelers on the path of recovery is to help one another find and hold fast to our uniqueness while sharing our own special power each of us has to increase our success and the success of each other. Let us make a new pact and add the power our new friends bring to share as we march forward together as warriors for addiction freedom. Please join hands with your fellow warrior to prepare for our journey tonight."

I joined hands with Arnie on my left and Beverly on my right. After a few moments to give us time to get joined up Paul began the only thing I was certain of so far as being a usual part of recovery meetings, a prayer. With the voice and tone of a well-seasoned preacher or minister, which I am sure he was or should have been at this time from his poise and grace of speaking I was seeing and hearing. He closed his eyes, bowed his head, and began to pray with the familiar first verse of the AA Serenity Prayer: "God grant me the serenity..." he spoke it and I and most others said the words of the complete short prayer out loud with him.

Those few verses most everyone who hears them assumes are in the Bible. They actually are not. A minister named Reinhold Niebuhr originated it and it was spread through his ministry and adopted by the Alcoholics Anonymous organization and has traveled the world over. It was for me and I guess every other person recovering from addiction, something we heard in our very first meeting and are told we should pray it at least once every day thereafter. I do but it's not the only prayer I know or pray each day or every day. Because the AA experience and plan of recovery is considered a spiritual journey, prayer is the essential ingredient of recovery right behind abstinence.

From the point where the Serenity Prayer was spoken and ended, nothing followed at The Fisherman's Net that I or anyone who has gone to a sponsored AA or NA recovery meeting would expect. We did share that we were once addicted to something and how long we had been clean, but that was where any real similarity ended. Yes, it was still largely about addiction and recovery. No, we didn't disavow, or deny, disobey, or go against any of the predominant truths about the tragedy and destruction of addiction that AA, NA, and the host of other recovery organizations hold fast to. But what we did do was discover that there were better ways to perceive the reasons for our addiction and the addiction itself. Equally important we discovered and learned that how we believe and what we believe about the very words addict, addiction, detox, treatment, and recovery, are critically more important than we usually thought because we had only a cursory understanding of them unique to our own experiences.

In two and a half hours Paul, who was not an ordained minister, showed us how to look and see beyond our own personal isolation as weak and broken ex-addicts struggling to rebuild our lives. He opened minds and poured in a new way of thinking and perceiving what addiction was and why believing we alone were responsible for our addiction slowed or prevented recovery and well-being and happiness. He and his wife joined us together as warriors with a common cause to help each other liberate our higher power. We discovered new ways of defeating the stigmas of addiction that proclaimed us as weak-minded, weak-willed, selfish people who cared little about what our abuse of drugs or ourselves did to others. He opened doors to new worlds that revealed we could be strong and powerful in shaping our present and our futures by transcending our isolation and building trust bonds with others to lighten our burdens and share our struggles. Our own unique but united 'higher power' was God in the Holy Spirit. We each joined our brothers and sisters in that room and joined together through the Holy Spirit to an Almighty God of the universe.

What he did not do, and what Shauna demonstrated to us we should not do either through a very comedic demonstration unique to being black and being an ex-addict, was lose our focus on the present, the here and now, the immediate. I certainly, and most others there that night saw for ourselves by sharing our self-perceived strengths and weaknesses one at a time, what WE DID was more important to our recovery than what we were thinking about our recovery. Each of us experienced the power of learning from one another's unique and common life struggles. The magic, if there was any that night was discovering how working together in small groups with people you could build trust bonds with, can continuously magnify the individual's power, the small group's power, and the big group's power. I saw for myself as others did, this reality doesn't just apply to the school classroom for straight people or big business or government think tanks, it did work and can work, for addicts or ex-addicts and recovery.

Everyone contributed or demonstrated something important and useful that night and for a few, I included, we saw beyond our stigma of being an addict, the uniqueness of self as a positive and valuable component of a society. We were each warriors that night in a battle for survival against formidable odds that had previously defined us as the ills and the problems of family, a neighborhood, a community, and the world at large. We did, as Paul told us we could and wanted us to believe we would transcend the world of the addictions and failed recoveries, our old world and all of its deception and distortion, and arrived into a new dimension of self-empowerment and group values, that had a harmony of belief and purpose. For some it was obvious it was a powerful new reality they had always wanted to be a part of.

To this very day I believe if we had spread across the country the twenty-five individuals who were in those five groups of five, we could have changed the entire spectrum of recovery and made recovery a beneficial and powerfully aligned partnership of forces. Because everyone had contributed or demonstrated something important and useful that night, myself included. We saw beyond our stigma of being an addict AND ITS LIMITS, the uniqueness of self as a positive and valuable component of a society. I can only pray that new reality is one everyone there that night stays in and help others to discover.

One important aspect of becoming a regular at the Friday meeting was learning critical information about a different recovery topic in depth. It was essentially outpatient therapy of an advanced type wherein one member of the group chose or was given a topic to become the 'expert' on before the next meeting. The topics and the person opting to become the expert was guided by Paul's wife, who had a Master's degree in Social Work-MSW, and the 'expert' would develop some kind of a skit, dramatic or comedic, alone or with others as players to perform. At the meeting described above the topic was discrimination. Shauna, who was black, and Phan Van, who was a Vietnamese guy playing a traffic cop, put us in stitches with a funny but painful routine about a traffic stop and the realities of stereotyping and racism. It illuminated the problems of language barriers and belief systems and how common but erroneous beliefs and not being perceived beyond being an ex-drug addict in recovery stifles personal growth and interpersonal relationships.

We took a break after the routine which had been preceded by Paul's thirty-minute exploration of Transcendental Meditation and how we could each benefit from some of the premises it was based on. Most everyone struggling in the early stages of recovery has a serious need for productive time structure and learning how to keep a wandering and tempted mind engaged and a body recovering from the physical effects of prolonged drug use. TM is a good basic discipline for some needing to find a consistent path to learning or relearning consistent focus and limiting the urges to use. I did follow his advice and read some of the articles and books on the subject he shared with us.

We took a break and enjoyed fellowship and abundance more like a church social than a recovery meeting. Some members and donations the members had put together the food and drink that went well beyond any meeting before or since. Paul had converted the idea of a meeting into a social learning lab and a sports bar. He applied business acumen to it and got everyone involved in outreach for support and they were incredibly successful at it. Most of us took the twenty-minute break and socialized, exchanged phone numbers, outside interests and activities, and the like. When the break was over we formed up into groups of five and Paul assumed the role of the teacher in a classroom standing in the middle of our groups and had us read and discuss the topics on a three-page handout. Ninety minutes of the best and most intense discussion of topics focused on better ways of seeing through the maze of misunderstandings about ourselves and the world we lived in than I could have imagined. It was fast and furious and oh so productive. When it was over we were tired and one hell of a lot more perceptive about our capacity to change what needed change and ignore what really didn't matter in our lives.

In sporadic conversations that I had with Arnie since that crucial and life-changing Friday night meeting I almost didn't go to, I learned some of the interesting histories that made Paul and the Fisherman's Net experience possible for me. Paul was a serious believer and practitioner of TM and gave credit to it for overcoming his own short but scary addiction. Even though he had basically grown up in a church environment, remember his father had converted the not real Sandy Cove Church into the real thing with Paul helping him, that alone did not provide a barrier to addiction happening. He had gone away to college and the military and had left behind a life where he was regularly standing on the preacher's stage reading as an adolescent and teenager Bible passages to his family and friends. He returned to the Sandy Cove area bringing home a new wife and started a successful business and a fall from a ladder fixing the old church's roof changed his perception about drugs. Because of his own personal eye-opening experience with prescription meds he had chosen to donate his free time for the last five and a half years to various kinds of addiction outreach.

Paul and his friends and followers altered my own path and I continue to hear about some of them and believe one person with a good idea can change the world. Even though Paul was neither an ordained minister nor a licensed drug counselor, his knowledge and understanding of people and addictive behaviors, and even God was far more credible and useful to me personally than any specialist in the fields that I have yet to encounter. I have sat in the Psychiatrists offices that were far more effective in relating precise solutions to my difficulties correcting the broken relationships with my children and family. I have been to NA meetings that made me see my problems were no different and no more unique than most other addicts or ex-addicts. I have set in a pew in church and listened to a sermon that moved me to tears that I will never forget. But what one man with a plan and a handful of human resources could achieve with a dynamic approach to growing ME beyond my addiction was unique and made the greater difference in me. It was the How we did together, what we did, that made it the therapeutic soul-expanding experience it was.

A little comic relief could go a long way in the smoky rooms to make an AA or NA recovery meetings more than a twelve-step reality check of the hardship and struggle that each of us is going through away from the fun and excitement of the world we are no longer much a part of.

We get but temporary relief from the necessity to open up painful memories, or share the hurt and disillusion each of us as ex-addicts experience daily, putting one foot in front of the other walking the straight line. For both of us, the non-addict and the addict alike, temptations abound out here in the everyday world to drag us into addiction. For the one, as Paul pointed out, it's perceived at the moment as a mysterious and intriguing step forward in our life adventure to try just once, for the other it is a familiar step back into the big trap of destructive hell. Every day there are fewer and fewer places you can go and enjoy being with others that doesn't overwhelmingly parade right in front of us all means and methods to addiction for the one and relapse for the other. Parties and celebrations, bars and clubs, concerts and festive street events, so many venues where normal social interaction takes place to pose subtle but powerful attraction into addiction traps for the unwary or direct threats to recovery for the other. What is too often left for us in recovery is the smoky rooms and the like where sharing hardship and sadness is the main event we go to be part of. It's not fun, exciting, glamorous, and by anecdote or statistics, it really isn't that productive when measured by rates of success. We got detoxified for the moment, thrust into a disjoint treatment program, told to be careful and cautious, attend meetings, but did anyone really believe we were Free'd from the true subtle causes of addictive habits taught to us? I say no, it is still too little, and more change is decidedly needed as addiction and addiction death increases exponentially.

As the old saying goes; if we repeat the same thing over and over again expecting a different result, isn't that insanity, the well-worn truth proclaims? Is it really hard to see why being alone and loneliness are both a huge part of addiction and its secrets? Isn't the dilemma posed clear and obvious not much has changed and more and more we fail time and time again? Isn't it a little more obvious upon close honest scrutiny why an entire generation, and now two, of vulnerable youthful bright futures, left unguarded and unwise about the increasing deceptions imposed upon them without their consent, fell into the Big Trap? Before they get beyond grade school age they are bombarded and then not many years later targeted, by deceptions of glamour and excitement of alcohol and intoxication. How could anyone believe there is no connection made in our youth that intoxication in and of itself is just a wonderful way to have fun alone or with other people? It's absurd to deny the very basis for addiction to harder more destructive substances isn't being made acceptable by proxy.

The second and third years in the rooms provided insights and a different way of seeing my own journey up the twelve-step ladder as a process even non-addicts could benefit from. I was seeing in myself and others there were hidden things in each of us that largely laid the foundation for our abusive habits or our addiction tendencies. Responses to abuse and fears acquired in our childhoods, faulty relationships with parents, siblings, peers, a variety of unresolved conflicts and secrets we kept or hid from. No, I wasn't unique at all and my real problems were not actually substance abuse, they were for the most part symptoms or responses to issues in each of our hearts and minds that didn't have answers or answers we were comfortable with or couldn't accept. Substance abuse was just a new issue of its own adding more obstacles to success and fulfillment in our lives. And oh how much was I slapped in the face by what was right in front of me for so long that I just wasn't connecting the dots on. I had seen a few glimpses in out-patient therapy with Dr. Pat that helped me along but not like I was seeing now four years clean and meeting and counting.

LOVE. Giving, receiving, or sharing love I was not in any way alone the one person who was confused by LOVE at all. My what a flash it was one night driving home from a meeting way out in the boondocks at a church with crosses on all four walls with Jesus looking down at me from them all! Not everyone I had listened to in that meeting or any meeting had it all figured out about love and could make me understand the good and the bad. Just the opposite was true enough that the majority of us, we should call LOVE or the lack of it, or misunderstandings about it, our common denominator! Because it was and I was certain of it like I had never been certain before this night. LOVE.

Even my Higher Power was demonstrating it in real-time! Indeed I understood in a bright flash in my mind on a poorly lit road that was supposed to be a shortcut back home but wasn't, so many of us myself included, had traveled down the wrong road. And unfortunately for some... more than once. A road full of potholes, missing direction signs, and ultimately a dead end, had broken my heart as a child, my romantic notions in my tender teenage heart, and finally, my adult belief about bonds and fidelity within a marriage, and ultimately had taken away almost forever my entire basis and my desire to trust any human or a human promise.

Meeting after meeting share after share reveals after reveal I was hearing with words and without words the dilemma of love and trust in the smoky rooms. Feelings of pain and despair, broken promises, broken hearts, broken minds, broken relationships, broken, broken, and broken. And finally, we all found another broken promise that our substance of choice had broken its implicit promise to make it all better if only for a little while. So here we were gathered together to share the story of broken. After we shined a light into the dark place we each kept our own broken, we walked step by step together sharing the light to illuminate the recovery journey we were taking one meeting one day at a time. Some of us had more oil in our lantern and we shared that quality of mind or heart with those that had less or were weary and fallen. We shared our strengths to make each other strong and fulfill a purpose, a plan, a hope, or a dream, and yes a promise we made, but always in helping others, I discovered more about whom I was and who I was always becoming.

As is spoken, "not my will Lord but Yours..."

8

A Smokey Room Brawl

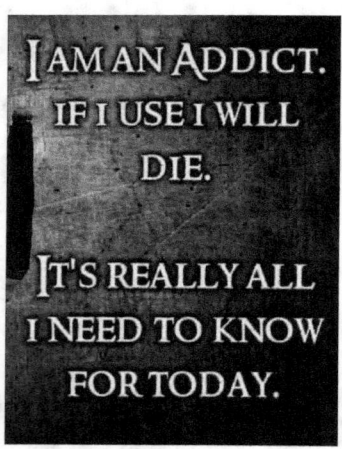

Let's chat about some of the other smokey room adventures this recovery path took me on. I was befriended by a young girl named Nikki at a meeting close to my house on a Monday at the Crestwood Community Center. Nikki was barely twenty-one years old with a long family history of substance abuse and addiction and critical conflicts were arising in her relationships and asked if I could help her in resolving them before they got any worse. We began chatting on the phone almost daily and discovered we had some common family history that heavily influenced our choice to abuse alcohol as teenagers. I was happy to have someone to talk to and a young female who could give me some feedback on ideas I had about rebuilding my relationship with my daughter Crystal. I could relate with much of her story seeing we had made similar choices at times of great distress for teenage girls and we had both made choices about men a few years later when alcohol heavily clouded our judgment. Our emotional maturation was insufficient to the task of choosing the right life partner amidst dancing and loud music on hot summer nights. When Jared boldly introduced cocaine into our two-year-old marriage he had already so subtlety undermined my womanhood, and made me so eager to make our relationship and marriage work at almost any cost, I didn't have enough foresight or the right guidance to slam the brakes on for myself and let go of the relationship. Had only a year or two more passed before the coke happened I would have had the emotional and mental maturity to resist further submission and avoided total destruction. I am certain today had I not felt shameful about losing my virginity to rape, and so insecure about my dark family secrets, and had just a little more courage and self-esteem as a secure adult woman, addiction would have never occurred.

I was determined to open up Nikki's thinking to explore her own personal values and choices for her to make better decisions than I did. Her personal integrity was being challenged and the intermittent drug use she was participating in was only likely to escalate if she didn't escape the trap she was naively walking into. I think this is where the need to help others emerged believing my own choices were not unique and I could assist those open to guidance from someone who had already been where they were going. I believe my desire to help others avoid tragedy ahead and help them overcome bad choices with good decisions was something valuable I could retrieve from my own experiences. If I could influence just one person to avoid the drugs altogether, or pull just one person from certain destruction ahead, or walk just one person through recovery, I could validate my own ten-year addiction on the street as more than something I must forget and gain nothing from. I became determined, with loving prompting from the Lord, to share what I learned finding my salvation that cleared my path of dysfunctional beliefs impeding my growth that resulted in hard addiction. I steadily felt more positive as years flew by about my choices and accepted I would continue to improve my ability to help others find answers and solutions and gain insights and understanding of our common plight. It was further set into my soul to be proactive in reaching out when it felt right as Nikki and a few others assured me I was instrumental in guiding them to adopt positive attitudes about their struggles and move solidly ahead in their recoveries.

Nikki did very well in her recovery journey believing she had within herself seeds of greatness. She worked with fervor and determination to raise herself up from mediocrity she had surrendered herself to, and went off to college majoring in social work to be of all things a therapist and recovery specialist! I and her cadre of friends and supporters wished her well departing from the last meeting with us in the smoky room adventure we shared. We assured her, she never had to willingly submit to anything substance abuse was even a small part of and not to let anyone stop her from achieving her dreams.

The relationship with Nikki and the ones that followed increased my level of commitment to being a friend to those needing someone to trust and be guided by. I had faith that where I had been, where I was, and where I was going, would ultimately negate my addiction experiences as permanently impairing my mind as I once accepted they had. I had largely avoided serious emotional commitments or permanent relationships with people my entire life until reaching a point in my emotional maturity with an accurate perception of the human condition that I believed was reliable enough to offer critical and applicable guidance. Because unresolved shame issues led me into increasing levels of self-isolation as I aged and traveled down the addiction path, I lacked the life insights necessary to validate my own personal development and stable character integrity. My fears had robbed me of developing normal interpersonal skills and the confidence I needed to interact well with age or workplace peers. Thus I became even shyer and introverted furthering the isolation leaving me largely emotionally impaired ad infinite. I neurotically feared that if anyone were to discover the ugliness of my childhood and the tragic events of molestation and rape I naively believed were somehow my fault, or I dared share my truth of the emotional and physical abuse in a dysfunctional marriage I endured believing my female inadequacies were responsible for, I would be rejected even more. Only time, therapy, and devoted self-directed study of the psychology of living in the modern world over many years ultimately free'd me of limiting and self-defeating beliefs.

The journey of self-discovery had begun some time back and was well underway and I was replacing the impairments with knowledge and experience and trusting in the direction my higher power God was leading me.

Maria was a hard-working gal with two boys from two different marriages, one thirteen and the other three. The youngest one left her crying all the time unable to explain why daddy didn't stay with them or why he rarely came to visit. Her soon to be Ex, Ricardo, was a Meth addict, and his attitude and erratic behavior slowly destroyed their family stability, but she continued trying to get him help so he could learn how to help himself and they could raise a family together. She could not fathom how he could continue choosing meth over his family she confided to me and asked if there was something wrong with her or was she doing something wrong? At first, she was resistant to my suggestions that some but not all of what she was hearing within this particular meeting group wasn't really steering her in the right direction. She needed to believe she was capable of success for herself and her kids on her own if that was what must ultimately be the choice.

    The Oaks meeting attendance averaged about thirteen with as few as nine and as many as eighteen I had seen in attendance. It was predominantly male with only five super regular females including myself. There had been as many as eight gals but two of them I had casually befriended struggled with job schedules and babysitter issues and one wasn't so certain she could stay clean. There were a few sad stories but this was a group with strong opinions and more than a few outrageously funny stories were shared. I learned in the first few meetings that all but one of the regular guys, Andy, was in active relationships with non-using female partners. Andy's tale of woe was his ex got him hooked and left him when the money ran out and he decided to go straight. We got a candid laugh with him when he shouted "No more wild women for me!" Tommy, the youngest of the group had just turned twenty-one, had a forty-four-year-old sugar mama supporting him and his coke habit for three years until she caught him two months ago in bed with the nineteen-year-old addicted sister of his dealer. According to his tacit admission, "I got to attend these meetings and stay straight and be a man worthy of her for six months till she humps me back, oops, I meant takes me back." A few of the guys thought it was humorous and laughed but I don't think the females, myself included, laughed at his macho stud self-image knowing he was an immature jerk with a vanity minded enabler. Sad, but maybe he would stay straight get a job to grow up, and be a real man.

    The gals were all ex-addicts with casually using or never used male partners except Ellen, who had a female partner who had been clean for almost a year. The mostly under thirty guys had kind of bonded in a belief that women simply could not understand the forces that kept their men using. Their shared attitude revealed that these so-called forces included covert implications that their women were rejecting them as men and the men's natural right to a sovereign leadership and authority was being withheld from them. This weakened them and further strengthened their urge to use for which the women were then part of the problem not a part of the solution to their drug use. The dominant attitude they had slowly united in was so clearly wrong and counter-productive I almost stopped attending the group completely believing the mindset could not be diverted long enough for the group to achieve anything but time structure and a bully pulpit for the men who were ticked off they didn't still have enablers sitting at home waiting for them.

I skipped three of the twice-weekly meetings at Crestwood believing going there was mostly a waste of time but in the dark, in prayer, my higher power illuminated my strength in a will greater than mine. Though I didn't understand the urges I was feeling that compelled me to return to the group, at the next Monday meeting when I was comfortably settled in for the sixty minutes of mellow drama that I was expecting I saw the group had a new dynamic. The ratio tonight was evenly divided between male and female and we had lost one of the more boisterous chests beating Tarzan types and gained some new souls. The girls were the same ones I already knew save the two new ones, but we had gained a tall older guy about forty physically fit and pretty good looking who appeared to be the alpha male type by his body language and the casual self-assurance in which he conversed. I kind of sensed Merle was going to remain the quiet type who would come and go having not gone much beyond introductions and maybe a tiny bit of small talk, the meeting is little more than a place to be for an hour and be reminded he was in recovery. My earnest hope was he wouldn't be another tribal type with an easy-to provoke antifeminist attitude. I hoped one day I would understand the conundrum that they loved us for our boldness in the kitchen and the bedroom but hardly anywhere else?

There are occasionally big differences between the smoky room procedures group to group that can make for good use of recovery time that have rules, a leader or a senior sponsor guiding our recovery discussions and planning events. Apparently, the week before my first meeting at Crestwood the Chairperson and meeting manager, an older gentleman with eight years of sobriety, had a work accident and remained in rehab for his injuries and would not likely return for another month. The Chairperson had two guys who he was sponsoring in attendance and they dominated to some degree what we were doing largely ignoring the Step guidelines the sponsor had provided them with, I learned. Their best contribution in my opinion was they made the coffee we drank and cleaned up when we left.

The Crestwood recovery group meeting began and ended with the normal prayer and between these points progressed along with whoever wanted to share something just doing so and the rest of the group members just weighed in on the issue being shared. One attendee picked a Step or Step topic, or question for discussion and everybody put in their two cents worth until everyone who wanted to share on the topic had done so. Another attendee would do the same thing until the meeting was over. Round Robin someone at another room called it. Illuminating the differences in male and female views is often encouraged in NA and can be a good learning experience for understanding differences in male-female perceptions on critical issues. But for it to work in a meeting or really anywhere it had to proceed equally and needed some kind of order and fairness maintained. A minority of two grew to five over a few weeks taking unchecked forays without a chairperson controlling presence steadily subverting the meeting's rules of order leading to unproductive emotional debacles.

Unfortunately, one of the assertive me Tarzan you Jane types spoke up first another of his tribe member friends supported him and they provoked one or all of the girls and the meeting became an unmediated debate between male and female views on any topic. At my seventh visit, it ultimately followed the same old pattern pitting a male anthem of rightful supremacy against the female orthodoxy of equality and personal responsibility. I finally decided I would join in the fray and speak up after the other girls, who were always more open and self-assured and willing to stand their ground than I was, became exasperated and suddenly quit the battle in agreement conceding defeat to immature male ignorance. I was going to say something that I hoped would get support to redirect the Tarzans away from blowing up the meeting again for everyone else. We were about thirty minutes into what started as a good meeting centering on the Fourth Step, talking about past mistakes and admitting to our faults and such. It got lopsided and some angry looks from me and the other gals when one of the newbie guys started ranting about women usually being more at fault for getting men hooked, keeping them hooked, getting hooked, being hookers, he went all over the place with his every woman is an aggressive accomplice in the downfall of man chants. Quick and cutting his verbal tirade revealed a misogynist who didn't stay in detox long enough or skipped it altogether and came here with powerful cravings still running wild in his system and on display for anyone to see.

Of course, Andy and Tommy had to follow his lead with a few quick cynical one-liners as Tarzan's thumping their chests in conquest over the female species in the kingdom of phallic giants. A few had left early at the previous meeting and now most everyone here was completely riled up in less than five minutes of verbal chaos. It was certain a lot of them were going to leave now this not being a recovery meeting anymore. I never figured out who it was, nor did anyone admit to me knowing who blurted out loudly, "Just Look At Connie!"

Connie had quietly shared with us during some earlier meetings why she was here and that she had stopped using over a year ago. She was candid in revealing her dejection about the inevitability of getting a divorce to protect herself and her children. Sadly her hubby was sitting at home getting high most nights making them broke while she was here at a meeting. Because she had gotten clean and he hadn't she should feel more responsible and stay married to the bum until he got clean… was the Tarzan tribes drumbeat advice to her after the previous meetings' probable divorce reveal. I was in total disagreement but that meeting ended before I could make any comments.

As the words 'Just Look At Connie' fell from the air tonight it went dead silent and the sound of a pin drop a mile away would have blown through the room like a bomb going off. I cringed with disgust feeling the emotional impact of the barrage of mindless accusations against all women directed at her. Anger welled up within rising like a powerful fountain and I leaned forward in my chair and turned toward her two seats down from me thinking I would shout out 'that's so cruel and so wrong' to challenge the malicious implication and let her see she would not be left exposed and alone to defend against ugly misguided accusations. The shy and soft-spoken woman who left the beaten addiction demon far down the road behind her, tirelessly coming here week after week in search of answers to save a marriage and a husband who would not fight the demon as she had, shrunk down in her chair face in hands and began softly sobbing.

Something in my head exploded. I felt a sudden searing flash of mental rage burning on my face as I bolted up from my seat to confront Andy and Tommy surrounded on either side by their like-minded friends. I thrust my arm out with finger-pointing like the barrel of a gun sighted between their eyes.

"Wait an f.cking minute! Shut your stupid mouth you arrogant asshole!" I screamed out eyes locked on Tommy believing he was the one who made the mocking cynical accusation about Connie. A dark raging voice of vengeance was telling me to rip his tongue out and kick him in the groin as hard as I could for his heartless cynical attack on a woman searching for help.

"What the hell do you know about relationships, you barely rate being a dog in heat you sick prick! You are nothing but a gutless dog bragging about your sugar mother like some kind of badge of honor to wear you sick f.ck!" It was a boiling fury that erupted from my soul and screamed the truth at him. The suddenness of my movements rising to attack them in a maniacal frenzy startled and froze them in place, eyes wide and fearful, a white-hot menace jumped from hell to attack them without forewarning.

"Tiffany please, please, please, it's alright!" I felt a hand of someone who was beside or behind me grab my arm and I snatched it free from the grasp but felt a hand from someone else land on my shoulder who mumbled something with another please that was unintelligible. I twisted and shook myself free of the hand trying to abate my rage. The angst building inside me for many weeks was finally vented in disgust and loathing of their very presence and hardened my resolve to force the menace they were from this place. Recovery meetings were a lot of things and confronting negative people sometimes had to occur but this was not the way any of us wanted to do it. My angry words alone might not be enough to end the wrong kind of confrontations they enjoyed provoking but this was not over, no it was not over but no one in the room could have expected least of all me, what happened next. That rush of compassionate tears that welled up from within me when I saw Connie's tears was a deeply powerful force joining her emotional helplessness with my own feelings of powerlessness to defend ourselves against the egotistical dominance of these pitiful locker rooms jocks forced upon us. Those few tears were gone and I was not about to sit down or shut up or run letting the disorder they were or the false shame they released on Connie reign unchallenged again.

I had their attention and that quiet power that was within me now was far greater in force than all the pain I suffered getting to this place in time. Andy held his stare toward me and started to rise from his chair as Tommy began to rise with him, eyes locked defiantly to mine, and whether one or both of them were thinking about coming at me I will never know. I did not see the first movement or it simply didn't register in my mind with all of me locked onto the target of my wrath Tommy had made himself, but the trap was sprung. Like an eagle diving on its prey, in a single swift motion, Merle rose from his seat at the end of the half-circle of chairs and come around behind and between the two of them putting one firm hand on each of their shoulders pinning them down forcefully into their seats. I saw on their faces a harsh grimace and heard twin gasps of pain as they began turning simultaneously to see who or what had locked onto them. Squirming to free themselves their movements stopped suddenly more curses spewing from Tommy's lips and they slumped further down as Merle leaned down close to their heads and spoke something I couldn't hear. Everyone in the room was now looking toward me or them with confused looks or little nods or shaking their heads uncertain of what had just happened in less than a minute maybe it was two who will ever really know.

I saw the tiny puddle of urine forming at Tommy's feet and the darkening discoloration of the crotch of his tan khaki slacks growing bigger and perceived vaguely the looks of a few changing as they too saw the evidence of fear and physical pain spreading on the shiny tile floor. I looked first at the hands clutching and holding fast in their chairs the degrading idiots and peered into the eyes of a virtual stranger that Merle was. When our gazes met it was a feeling of strength and assurance that calmed my mind and secured my actions. He barely nodded with an affirmation of support and I shifted my gaze back to his subdued prisoners and brought down my handgun and took two long steps to shorten the distance between us. Slightly beyond their possible reach if they lunged, which I hoped was in no way possible in Merle's powerful grip, I stopped and exhaled the breath my stealth was holding back to power the rush at them my instincts were preparing me to do.

All movement and conversation ceased when I stepped forward to commit whatever action I would. Each of us in this room together knew now at this moment the choice of their fate was ours and must play out to the end and whatever it was to be we were joined in a psychic collective to see it through. The value of weeks of days and hours of our lives and our respective journey joining for recovery were stolen and lost to egotistical male hubris we had endured... together, and together we would end the reign over our efforts by rebellious disrespectful children in our midst. I pulled in a slow deep breath and loosed the fleeting thought, 'Lord please forgive me.'

Andy was dejectedly staring at his shoes refusing to look at me or maybe he was looking at the tiny puddle of pee at Tommy's feet hoping he would not lose control over his own physical pain or emotions and be shamed in front of so many. "Look at me, you dog," I said slowly with deliberate livid emphasis word by word. A few tense moments ticked by Andy resisting my demands until I saw Merle's hand tightening his grip on Andy's shoulder and knew his thumb was digging deeper into the pressure point in the shoulder just at the base of Andy's neck. He let out a gasp and his head jerked up but he wouldn't look me in the eyes. It was enough. The fire in my head and the pain in my heart for Connie was subdued and I knew we were all just so tired of their asinine antics and verbal abuse the women were needlessly enduring. Most of the people present week to week had tolerated their mayhem with compassionate empathy that these two immature jerks were troubled souls struggling as were we with their own post-addiction issues. But they had knowingly taken it too far ignoring numerous repeated attempts to check their attitudes at the door for an hour and remember why the rest of us came to this room.

"Neither of you are men. You are nothing but whining little boys swinging your little pee-pees' around for attention. No sense of shame or decency stops you..."

"Let go of me you son of a bitch," Tommy hissed twisting and squirming trying to free himself from Merle's grip. He let out a deep moan of pain and stopped squirming and the color drained from his face as Merle applied even more force to the pressure point that held much longer would result in unconsciousness. Merle leaned his head down and spoke something into Tommy's ear loud enough that I was certain Andy could hear but too low for me to make out clearly. Whatever he said was enough to still them both and return their angry stares to my face. Merle raised his eyes to mine and flashed a quick smile and nodded his head affirming cooperation to his control and me their attention. He waited for a long moment and gave me another assertive little nod indicating he wanted me to continue. I had calmed sufficiently from my emotional assault to focus on what to do, or how to end the milieu our meetings had become, we each had too much at stake to allow it to continue, or let two childish jerks and their accomplices chase us away to other rooms.

I took a quick furtive glance around me taking in those behind or arrayed in front of me not pausing to look at any one person or look at their face. It was perceptible no one was moving or talking and all eyes were on me or Merle and his hostages. I turned and gave Connie a quick smile and returned my attention to our mutual adversaries moving a few inches closer and spoke slow and firmly.

"Both of you are going to apologize to Connie and ask her to forgive you. And then you are going to apologize to every woman in this room for all the garbage you have been spewing… and then you will apologize to everyone in this meeting. Maybe they will forgive you and maybe they won't… I don't know why they should because you don't respect anyone least of all yourselves or none of this would have happened. So you call your sponsor and tell him how much trouble you have caused and how sorry you are. You are not better or privileged because your sponsor was the Chairperson. You both think you're tough or special or whatever, but you aren't you are just weak and scared and hide behind an attitude. The rest of us came here to help each other and that included you, which apparently you don't give a damn about. We would help you but you don't want our help and I don't think you deserve it anymore either. But it's not up to me it's up to Connie and everyone else. So… you get it right? You got it and you'll do what you need to do, right?"

I was using every ounce of self-control I had to speak sternly without letting them see I was trembling like a leaf inside. My queasy gut wanted to retch up the coffee that was burning in my stomach and my throat felt like I had drank battery acid. But the angry defiant stares had become sullen dejection as I spoke and they nodded weakly in unison they got it. I was grateful Merle had kept them firmly in place because I was very much afraid Tommy would instantly pounce on me with revenge in his heart for the embarrassment and shame I had caused him if he could have. Andy was clearly feeling shame he knew he had earned when he cast a quick glance at someone standing quietly above him standing in judgment and any defiance he had left in him melted his manly demeanor into a scolded child wanting to hide under his chair.

I felt Connie grab my arm and I stepped back away from them as the tense silence broke and people started talking to each other and shuffling around where they were standing. Merle leaned his head in quickly between Tommy and Andy and spoke briefly to them and released his grip and stood back just a little but looked ready to grab one or both of them instantly if it proved necessary. Andy was the first to move and cleared his throat loudly a couple of times trying to get his mind around what he had to do. He nudged Tommy whose color was returning a little and the defiance was now a continence of confusion. They stood up slowly trying to ignore the little puddle at their feet.

"Okay Connie I really am sorry but I wasn't the one that said anything about you really I didn't, I think you are okay really I do and I didn't mean to make you cry, honest I didn't mean to I am not like that. Everybody, everybody, listen to me… I ain't a bad guy I just talk too much and I'm sorry for it. I won't ever come back here I won't. I am sorry," Tommy pleaded his innocence and his sorrow with all the sincerity he could muster under the stress he was obviously feeling. He was visibly shaken and drained and brought his hands up to his mouth suddenly and turned away trotting towards the bathroom.

"Me either Connie, I didn't say it. I heard somebody say it so it wasn't me and it wasn't Tommy either. But really I am sorry about all the trouble I caused or we caused. I am just really scared as Tiffany said. It's hard for me to be here and I slipped up a couple of times too and I am sorry about it to everyone. Everybody hates me for what I did when I'm doing the junk. And probably everybody should hate me now for being an asshole here like Tiffany said. I don't know where else to go but I got to go to meetings or I got nothing and nobody. Please Connie try to forgive me for whatever I did I am really sorry about it really and I won't ever let anything like this happen again ever. Really Connie I am so very sorry." Andy was visibly trembling and tears were appearing as his voice fell to almost a whisper. He held out his arms as if he wanted her to come into his arms and hold her... or maybe what he wanted was to be held? I felt just a little compassion for him realizing he was still a boy wanting to be a man and had not found his way there yet, but he would. He just had to want it. Andy turned away from Connie and looked slowly from face to face of everyone there before he crumpled down into his chair repeating I'm sorry, I'm sorry, between deep anguished sobs.

Connie clasped my arm and asked if I was okay. I gave her a nod and a confident smile. She smiled back and squeezed my arm a little harder before she spoke again.

"You didn't have to do that for me, Tiffany. It wasn't really what they said that... made me cry. It's just everything and I had a really bad day. I have to get away from Allan, all we do is fight anymore and I'm afraid I'll start using again if I don't. It's bad." I acknowledged her with a sad smile and asked if she was going to be okay. She nodded her head yes and did what I nor anyone would have really expected, walking over to Andy still softly crying and rocking himself back and forth, she knelt down in front of him and put her hands on his shoulders. Only a woman with deep compassion and self-assurance can display courage and mercy in the way she did with her act of loving acceptance. She began speaking quietly to him and I knew she had within her forgiveness the power to lead Andy into a brave new world where his true manhood was patiently waiting for him to arrive.

I stood motionless for a long minute alternately watching Connie restore Andy's shattered pride, and staring at Merle who was leaning against the wall across the room now hands behind his back quietly taking it all in. Everyone began drifting out and a couple of guys started grabbing up the chairs while Carmen and one of the new gals started clearing the refreshment table and the coffee pots. Ellen, the gal sitting beside me when our little conflict erupted, emerged from the ladies' room near where Merle was leaning against the wall and was walking toward me with an ear-to-ear grin. She reached out her arms and gave me a big warm hug.

"Girl you are one badass! I was gonna jump in and help you waylay those guys but it seemed real quick you didn't need any help with Coach holding them boys down for you to kick some ass! I almost went to another meeting tonight cause I was tired of their macho bullshit, but hey, I wouldn't a missed this showdown no way! Girl you made us all look good tonight you and Coach," she said giggling and threw up her hand for me to return her high five. I did. "Thank you, Ellen. I am glad you are good with what I did. Maybe that wasn't the right way to get them to shut up but I was... well... what's done is done," I said.

"Aw right girl. I got to get goin' got some kids to put to bed. See you next time I guess," she said turning and headed to the door waving as she walked. Merle was still posed against the wall but gave me a big smile when our eyes met. I smiled back feeling a little awkward but decided I had to at least thank him. He had saved me from God knows what. Tommy could have knocked the hell out of me if Merle hadn't stopped him. A little shiver went through me. I walked across the room wondering what exactly I was going to say to him.

"Tiffany," he said smiling wide with an 'it's all okay' nodding of approval as I stopped and extended my arm offering up a handshake. In the back of my mind was the little reminder about repeating mistakes of the past. Indeed I felt the handshake almost insincere but giving him the big best new friend hug could send the wrong message... to both of us. Up close he had the magnetic appeal most women are attracted too and indeed that psychic connection established in the heated moments earlier was so kind of natural. I jerked my wandering mind back to the here and now of the moment.

"Merle... I uh... well many thanks for saving my ass! I am so – so sorry I got so worked up and started screaming at Tommy. It just happened. I lost it when Connie started crying... she's got enough problems already without those jerks blaming her for being a woman I guess and making her ashamed of anything... and no way did I want to get anybody else involved or you for God's sake," I said apologizing the best I could.

"Hey, it's okay, really. And there's no need to apologize, those guys needed a lot more than what you gave them Tiffany, and really did you hear anyone yelling at you to stop? I didn't. What I saw were a lot of people wishing it would have happened sooner than it did! Hey, maybe you should look at it like you helped them see the error of their ways!" he laughed and shook his head and when he looked me in the eyes again it was clear he was sincere about what he believed, he wasn't just being kind and letting me off the hook for what I had done.

"Thank you, Merle. I don't know what to do now, I don't mean right this minute because I am going home write all this stuff down in my journal because it's something I probably won't ever forget. But where does this meeting go? What's going to happen with Tommy and Andy and their sponsor, is this still going to be a meeting place without a Chairperson?" I asked. Merle flashed that big broad smile again cocked his head and pointed a finger at me.

"Well, you know you could be the Chair Tiffany, I am sure everybody here would vote for you," he answered wryly. I couldn't help but laugh at his quick wit. It wasn't anything he likely meant seriously but I had no way of knowing what he knew or didn't know about how NA meetings and Chairpersons were established but I did know it wasn't going to happen even if I was interested in being a meeting Chair. Not anytime soon anyway.

I responded to his humor with my own putting a mock-serious

thoughtful look on my face and pointed a finger up into the heavens and then at him. "Well, certainly. That's what my act was all about, getting everyone's attention to my calm demeanor and diplomatic way of doing things? It was obvious wasn't it that I have lots and lots of self-control!" He looked me in the eyes shook his head and busted out laughing and I lost my mock seriousness and laughed with him. We almost got to tears before we stopped.

I was feeling a little more assured about tonight's showdown not being viewed by him as something of a female temper tantrum. I was confident too there was a certain amount of respect he felt for me that I was honestly more concerned about Connie and others than my own personal desire to avenge their insinuations. His actions too were maybe more than just a chivalrous act to stop a fight. Tarzan-Tommy slapping Me-Jane senseless maybe was the not-so-funny image that flashed through my mind making me wince a little at the thought it could have played out just that way. But it was over now and I couldn't help myself from moving our little intimate interpersonal charade to the next level feeling there was something real and genuine we both felt standing here making light of a heated confrontation that he had been dragged into. Something neither one of us came to the meeting expecting tonight, but maybe we were just like normal people seeking like-minded friends and maybe a kindred soul we could share friendship with.

"Oh be serious Merle! You have no fear of me getting in the way of you being crowned the new Chair and absolutely you have my vote of confidence you are the man for the job you are so deserving of it! Who else but little ole' you could restore calm and order without so much as lifting a finger?" I said trying to keep a straight face. But when he put both hands over his ears and started shaking his head side to side I couldn't hold back a big grin. It became a long hearty laugh when he thrust one finger in his ear and stuck another finger in his nose a tiny bit and rolled his eyes around like we had seen the crazy guy do in how many slapstick television comedies.

Our reverie of humorous exchanges had served its purposes breaking the last vestiges of angry disarray and stresses the long ongoing war of words and the unexpected altercation tonight had produced. We were largely back to being who we were, ex-addicts attending a meeting with others to support each other and our common goal of recovery. Five minutes, ten, was it twenty, I guess we weren't really counting, a lot had been said but much more was exchanged not being spoken, and what of the actions we each had taken? Two virtual strangers with an audience of onlookers now dispersed and themselves trying to find a perspective on the people and events we had experienced together over the course of weeks or maybe months for those who preceded my arrival at Crestwood. Merle and I had successfully, or so I believed, gotten a secret glimpse of the voiceless character inside the person reforming themselves sharing a twelve-step journey one meeting at a time of which tonight was something altogether uncertain and hazy. Yes, this meeting was over but was it really concluded for Merle and me, when a long moment of silent appraisal filled empty air, no more comedic wit left in the well, determining where we went from here. Was it our separate ways or had fate drawn us here to find each other perhaps, two ships sailing alone on a stormy sea called recovery and passing in the night under a brightly lit moon and a thousand stars revealing the presence of each other? In near-perfect timing right on queue, a long moment of awkward silence was ended by the twice flicker of the overhead lights drawing our attention toward the door as an elderly gentleman, not one of us, called out, "Time to go folks. Got to lock up."

"Okay," we said in unison. We walked to the door stopping long enough to thank the gentleman for his patience and told him goodnight and we walked in step out into the parking lot. After a couple of steps, Merle stopped turned to me, and asked, "Are you coming to the next meeting Tiffany?"

I stopped mid-stride and turned and said, "I don't know Merle. There are other rooms a little closer to my house but I have made a few friends here already and I am worried about Connie, and Maria and I share a lot of stuff too. But you know after tonight I don't know. I am going to pray about it. What about you and something else while I am thinking about it, Ellen called you Coach. What's up with that?"

"Ellen. Yeah. Well that's a whole other story and well she wasn't supposed to let on she knew me for reasons that are another story too. But I guess... Ellen... Ellie, my sister Christine calls her, Ellie is with my little sister. They are you know... together. Live together. Ellie didn't make it a secret here that she is a lesbian and personally I have absolutely no problem with that. I didn't know anything about my sister because up until about six months ago she was dating a guy I introduced her to almost five years ago after she divorced her college sweetheart Alex. We haven't really been that close the last few years. I didn't even know she had any kind of addiction problem until we met up to watch the NBA playoffs at a sports bar and she introduced Ellie as the person who helped her get clean. Anyway, the next thing I know they moved in together and she came out. What a surprise that was so close together. Anyhow, I was heavily addicted to painkillers for a couple of years after back surgery and got busted buying some Oxy from a narco drug dealer. Lost my teaching job at Weldon High School, yes I was coaching basketball and teaching Science. The rest you can probably figure out. Detox, outpatient rehab, just started doing the rooms, district manager now for a sports and outdoor retail chain. So... That's my story. And since I've told you mine tell me about you. What brings you here to play troublemaker Tiffany? I mean if you want to... it's okay if you don't."

"No, it's okay. There isn't much to tell anyway or not that you really want to know. I don't know if you were here the night I did my big reveal, but it's been five years for me next month. Moved here from a little town in Texas, I had a career going strong and got married to a local guy, anyway two years into the marriage he sticks coke under my nose and it was all downhill from there. I had never even heard of cocaine, I drank a little rum and smoked a little weed, but the demon grabbed me badly and I left him and my babies stayed high for ten more years. I got a few bumps and bruises but I'm doing pretty good now I think." I told him.

"Well I have been to a couple of different meeting places and you certainly don't look like a lady with a ten-year track record from the streets. I don't want to sound crass but the drugs have been pretty hard on some people I've seen lately with just a year or so doing their thing. But hey... gives you lots of reason to speak up and say what's on your mind in there for sure. Some of the ladies seem pretty tough-minded and just let them get away with the macho bull but you could tell they were glad you stepped up."

"Thank you, Merle, I appreciate what you did and I think you could really be a help to these guys if you come back. They are just being led around like little sheep and if you stepped up... Coach... you could change it. You know really I don't know what you've seen in other rooms you've been to, but meetings are not just a place to confess and work the steps, what we are supposed to do is help each other change, you know what I am trying to say... you could make a real difference. Not just here but any room every room needs a good leader to make it work and make a change. So don't just think about you here, and I don't mean that negatively, I mean well... isn't it just another classroom for kids with special needs?" I was staring him in the eyes. I believed now what he was really here to do was staring back at him wondering how he was going to help himself and would he help heal those who were in a different kind of classroom... the Lord's recovery classroom... and He was showing it to Coach.

Before he could look away or respond to my plea I ended our unspoken as yet avenue to danger. It was here and was opening its door to a mutual curiosity about all the 'what ifs' that were possible for two strangers drawn to one another by forces, not of their own choosing. A man and a woman had been thrown together into a crisis of degree forming a quiet but strong bond that was unforeseeable and unchallengeable. If left unchecked, could have its own destiny sealing our fate in its natural human course. But it is here where the discipline of prayers to our higher power reigns in our humanness and gives us that knowing in the twinkling of an eye and changes our course and makes the crooked way straight as promised. In that critical tiny moment of time the instant counter-intuitive choice was made so the true path I and Merle were to follow guided by that giver of divine law was chosen, I said, "Well it's late Merle and I have to go home... alone... and get some beauty rest for the big day tomorrow.

"It took a lot of cold wisdom and strength to follow through with choice words given to me. I took a quick two small steps away from him and extended my hand for a handshake when the powerful emotional instinct was to give him an honest and warm hug of friendship and gratitude for his actions and his presence tonight at Crestwood. The will of my higher power had given me dominion and authority over my natural human body and mind to keep sovereign my path from Merle's protecting him from me and me from him and our natural instincts and our human responses. I closed the door with a coolness he might not have been expecting but it didn't appear to offend his male sensibilities in any observable way. With a big smile that was in his eyes and his body language too, he shook my hand and told me goodnight and hoped he would see me again and we climbed into our cars and moved on with life. I know he was going to ask me for my phone number at a minimum but that little bit of forced hardness in my voice had deterred him from doing so. But there were a few little conflicts taking shape in my mind reminding me I had little power over what tomorrow might bring being not the only person in the world with dreams and unmet emotional needs... and desires.

9

Other Pitfalls in the Rooms

I didn't go straight home but instead took a small detour stopping first to get a small carton of milk to soothe the burning still lingering in my throat and stomach, and then to a small hedged park a few blocks from home I frequented on sunny days to read and write. I walked the perimeter to ascertain it was reasonably safe no one hiding in the dark to surprise a late-night visitor. It was empty at this late hour being almost nine-thirty p.m., there were no kids playing, no teenagers hanging out to smoke who knows what or some to do we all know what if they could. I was wickedly surprised a few months previous accidentally interrupting a foursome of lovers at this time of night when I stopped to rest on my return from the nearby 7-11 to get a loaf of bread. I went to my favored covered table to sit and ponder the emotional roller coaster this day had been. It seemed it was perhaps a culmination of thinking and events that stretched back almost two months about some critical choices I needed to make about my future and how my total recovery was proceeding. I thought I knew where I was, indeed I was almost certain I was but for the higher powers' guidance, a near master of my own destiny by disciplined choice and obedience.

Today's events had shaken me loose from that deceptively comfortable but still false illusion of power and total control over that path and my ultimate self-chosen destination.

It's kind of funny that most of us go to our first group meeting with preconceived notions about recovery programs. I did. The beliefs most have are as varied as the source from which they got their original ideas and there are a host of differences between the Twelve Step recovery programs of AA, NA, and almost a dozen other old and well-known programs and methods. Most come to that first meeting expecting it to be a lock-step approach and everyone sits in their seats and confesses their sins of abuse, listens to a sermon about the evils of the substance or habit and relapsing, and then the class is dismissed much like in the familiar public school domain. Well... I have been told by some intimately familiar with the originating programs of AA over eighty years ago to some degree that was true then with only a little variation. It is certainly not true in my experience in any of the nine major recovery programs I am intimately familiar with that deal with alcohol, substances and drugs, physical or emotional abuse, food, sex, pornography, shopping, domestic violence and now even the Internet addiction has its own dedicated prescriptive recovery.

I surprisingly gained something of value from every meeting I attended. Today was no different. It was not that uncommon for people who are passionate about what they believe or their own experiences that they will fight to make or defend them.

A meeting without a Chairperson or some control can actually do more damage than good, I had sat through the meetings at Crestwood as they disintegrated observing a single dominant male barely out of detox steadily build a following with an anti-feminine mindset week to week strong enough to defeat the gains offered and available from older wiser heads. Of all things I have learned being out of the trap and off the hamster wheel is that apathy is contagious, dangerous, and destructive. The most valuable insight I learned in the smoky room meetings about myself, and for the most part, all other females who have suffered addiction problems of one kind or another are how easily we are doomed by our own brand of apathy. In my own experience, I was apathetic to a husband I trusted to protect me who all but shoved a substance I had never heard of up my nose. I was apathetic to his repeated infidelities bringing hookers home to our sacred bed. I was apathetic to twenty years of submission to that white fire cocaine that destroyed all but the last physical breath that the Lord hooked me to Himself with and mercifully snatched me from the grave I had fallen into. Yes.... apathy is deadly.

Observing, listening, sharing, crying, and laughing with more than a hundred and twenty other females in recovery illuminating sad despairing revelations about our experiences as women, and as addicted women, or caring for someone addicted who was a woman, has formed ninety-nine percent the entirety of my belief structure and value system that is my life and the way I live it. That integrated matrix of thinking and decision making, my personhood, is governed and was often supplied by my Higher Power, the loving God, and Lord Jesus Christ that I believe in and lovingly obey. Even when I struggled for a time with the precepts of a God or omnipotent being or presence, in or out of a Twelve Step program, which I think even that was given intentionally to me by my Higher Power to clarify my perception of real truth, apathy revealed itself and took the life of someone I loved. Apathy is the major direct attributable cause for the death of tens of millions the world over throughout history. The depth of the well of apathy and human suffering is far deeper and its origins precede written history and dwell in the oral traditions of our most ancient ancestors. I sat in a meeting this evening where that apathy was rearing its ugly head... and acted to end it.

No recovery meeting should be guided by apathy, and that was partly the reason I stopped at the park. To ponder a series of events and thinking the last few weeks and today had given me and guided my decision about returning or abstaining from Crestwood and what to do about my relationship with Kurt. The morning had been particularly trying owing to the ongoing battle with my disability but it was looking like it was going to be worked out very soon. There had also been a silly difference of opinion with Kurt that became a real argument of a kind we had never previously had. It didn't make much sense to me at 10:00 a.m. in the morning, but in light of the Tarzan's attitudes at Crestwood and what was finally obvious to me about men's general perceptions about a woman's value beyond the kitchen and bedroom, I had gotten a possible insight about Kurt and our relationship when I was wondering what I would say to Merle after he released the jerks.

I was at a crossroads today, and the encounter with Merle at a deeply personal level had brought it into focus. The steady diet of outpatient therapy when I needed it, the smoky rooms when I needed them and when they became my classrooms, and two well-worn library cards and sixty volumes had largely remade me. My recovery was going as good or better than I had expected or even thought, but there were always new challenges to meet. I believed I was at a level of understanding about my childhood and family relationships, my relationship with my own children, my identity and role as a mate but not a wife to Kurt, and perhaps most importantly, my own growth into a stable identity as a mature enough woman for my age, to be extremely satisfied with who I was now and my place in the world.

My role as a friend and guide to my fellow recovery travelers was deeply satisfying and fulfilling because I could see and feel the positive contributions I was making. I was freely given by many the extremely valuable feedback and suggestions that sharpened my perceptions and increased my knowledge about what I got right and what I didn't. But the very tiny little thing nagging at me today was the goal I had begun my recovery journey on, namely becoming an independent self-sustaining person living on my own. Kurt and I had agreed upon that premise when I came home with him leaving addiction and its misery behind me.

The reveal sitting here in the darkness delaying going home to Kurt was pretty clear and direct. The relationship we shared was becoming tempestuous more frequently as my recovered attitude changed my behaviors and in turn, changed my personality. My steady discipline to remain curious, to study, to learn, and to observe, had integrated knowledge and perception which resulted in a quiet but not shy, secure within myself woman, who could and did think for herself and embraced life as an equal to anyone I would encounter anywhere any time if I chose to do so. There were those above me in intellect and authority and I respected their stature, there were those below me living in unhealthy fear and apathy, and as often as they allowed I reached out to help them and prayed with them too. There was me and everyone else in the middle on the same plane in the same paradigm and I prayed for all of us to be all we could be.

It was going to rain very soon and I was feeling tired but I had time to think things through sitting alone in the park. It was clear in the simplest of ways Kurt and I had grown apart and steadily moving away from each other. Not by choice, but by our personal choices and their consequences. Maybe he missed the eager to please street girl whose every wish was my command in the bedroom and out. But he still liked my cooking as he had taught me well. Maybe he missed the insecure little house mouse afraid of the dark or even a stranger's too-long look. I simply wasn't that insecure beaten-up little girl anymore. I was me and I was very happy to be me every day even when the bones hurt and my head throbbed on a rainy cold day. The meeting rooms and the journeys I shared with many had enlarged my worldview and increased my interpersonal skills, perceiving what was real and what a maladaptive role was and I didn't want to play that part anymore and didn't. I had the courage to change for the better all I could and the serenity now to accept as it was all the rest. And thankfully most everyone agreed the new me was the best me yet. Kurt had lost his way after he got out of the service with PTSD, but I had pushed, pulled, and shoved till he got the help he needed and made him a better man in a lot of little brave steps. He attended his own smoky rooms for Vets and Vets with PTSD for a couple of years and made some new life-long friends. It changed him a little at a time until he found a new comfort zone. Silenced by time and understanding the sounds of battle were put in a box and locked away but what remained was the honor of being a duty-bound soldier in a war for those still crawling and those not yet born. Everyone, his family included, said the new Kurt was – the best Kurt.

He liked what he used to hate and hated what he formerly claimed he loved. I guess I fit in that equation now and he doesn't like the answer he is left with. His masculine fantasies fulfilled he was left bored to fantasy having someone to throw a ball with. In the quiet now was a time to be as a man again and not a soldier of valor saving a girl of the night from the dark and danger used and broken. The call of fatherhood was beckoning once again as the clock on the wall ticked and he was counting the days he had left to hear that first word called daddy again. I could go there again yes I was able, and gave it much thought I did, weighing the cost of being with child uncertain of the imprint that might be made, and what cost the womb could bear. Fears and tears, pain and shame, questions and answers no doctor could assure me. In the still of the early morning tomorrow before he rises to face another day of labor and toil I will testify to my choice both hands on my Bible to spare a good man from a threat unseen and a burden to carry not fair all the rest of his days. The decisions made, it was time to go home and leave the park until another sunny day. But I was certain now I would go back to Crestwood because there were people there I cared about and indeed some needed my guidance. I was nervous as hell when I arrived at Crestwood about twenty minutes early on Monday and Maria was standing outside talking with Ramona, a girl who was attending her first meeting at Crestwood tonight with her boyfriend Tony. After quick introductions by Maria, Ramona explained both were fresh out of meth detox about three weeks and on a monitored recovery plan so they could get their four-year-old little girl back from CPS custody. Her boyfriend Tony had met Maria's ex-husband Ricardo at a detox facility and learned about Crestwood and decided they would try it tonight. Ramona left us to find Tony who she nervously quipped hoped wasn't snorting in the bathroom he went off to find a few minutes before I arrived. It was obvious Maria was relieved when Ramona left because she said angrily, "That's the slut Ricardo was buying meth from."

I asked her how things were going with Ricardo. "Well about the same. He came home Friday and he said he was straight for a few days and he was going to make it this time because he really loved me and the kids. You know... I want to believe him but I heard it so many times before but I do care about him still and that's why I keep coming to these damn meetings. But Tiffany I tell you straight we are all glad you did what you did. It took guts." I thanked her for supporting my unusual way of doing things but I quickly shifted the conversation back to her. I explained to her that it wasn't that he didn't care for her he just loved his drugs more. I know it hurt her hearing me say that but I didn't think the advice she was getting in this group was helping at all. They told her just hang on and don't desert him because eventually, he will come around. All of which may be true and she had been doing so, but she wanted it now and didn't understand the rest of what was being said. He would have to 'want' recovery before it would ever work. Unfortunately the rehabs she kept paying for him to be in hadn't helped him get completely clean yet. It made it even worse that his parents blamed her constantly saying she wasn't being supportive enough and they believed if she would do more he would get clean.

"What more do you think you could do?" I asked her. "Can't you see he must want to recover for him to have the fairy tale life you're still dreaming about with him? How many more years can you go on like this giving of yourself before you fatally harm your sons by not being fully engaged in their lives?" I offered her a few more reality checks about the patterns Ricardo repeated each time she confronted his continuing drug use. I had hit the right spot to make her see the illusion she was enabling his drug use with. She just stood for a long moment squeezing her eyes shut hard against the tears that came and I gave her a reassuring hug to soften the dismay she was feeling. We got ourselves together and went in to join the meeting already in prayer both knowing she had ended her long denial and she was not the weak unsupportive mate others wanted her to believe she was.

I got a few nods and waves after the prayer was over and smiles from all the gals that were present at the showdown. I came back not knowing what to expect. I saw that neither Tommy nor Andy was there and Merle was absent too which kind of disappointed me.

In the months ahead the relationship between Maria and I continued to strengthen as I became the big sister she confided in guiding her to let go of the codependency she had accepted as being the best she could do. I was her sounding board for questions and the keeper of her secrets as she extricated herself from the mother role to a grown man who had to learn responsibility for himself, freeing her to be more than a scapegoat for his continuing addiction.

Maria flourished when the burdens of Ricardo's addiction baggage were left behind enabling her to find her way as a single mom successful managing family and career and a little more than a year after our first meeting was dating a guy who valued her and her kids enough to propose marriage. She told me recently how glad she was to have met someone who actually lived that life so she could understand the draw of addiction and how she had let Ricardo and his parents convince her to further enable him and avoid the truth about his addiction and the consequences.

One of my old sponsors reminded me when we were sharing similar news much like Maria's, to think the actions through to the end of the story before I made any rash short-sighted decisions about maybe enjoying the high just one last time believing I was really strong now and finally able to control the beast. That was probably the trick Maria was falling for with Ricardo and his wily excuses and then the blame his parents reinforced. Yes, it was a timely observation indeed because in most smoky rooms there are far too many opportunities meeting fellow souls attuned to the persistence of the urges to use who would readily draw you into the trap they had not fully free'd themselves from.

I had become perceptive and very adept at quickly spotting the guys and gals all too ready to share a connection to some 'really good stuff' if you wanted to meet up secretively after the meeting to go score. A self-destructive approach to life, indeed.

There are two types, maybe more but these followed consistent patterns I observed over many years. The most common were not long out of detox and more interested in getting high if they could find a way, then they were fully committed to their recovery. They were not always easy to spot across a room but a little friendly conversation they would engage you with after determining you were a means to an end would necessarily lead to the question of just one last high, wouldn't that be just the ticket tonight for you and me? The Hustlers I called them, were still running the hamster wheel from high to high and only running out of means for their next score had they found their way to detox and a room. More often than not the trip to detox was usually via a visit to jail first for whatever crime of choice they got caught committing. Drug sales or possession of a large quantity, theft, burglary, petty larceny, was on the rap sheet or addiction roadmap for the guys. I had heard or seen for myself all the most frequent routes leading to being in a smoky room telling your tale of woe. They were predators and dangerous if you were unsuspecting enough to be snared by the easy smooth talk that tickled the urge to use, you were here trying to control.

The gals were usually much less obvious and I had to observe more than body language and mannerisms to decide if they were here to recover or cruising this room and others 'looking for a driver.' The 'looker' was a description applied by one of my early sponsors to both guys and gals, she instructed me to avoid it if I wanted to stay clean. I thought it better fit the gals and I tagged them as 'Cruisers'. My sponsors, simple explanation was Cruisers weren't about recovery either and were not usually in any kind of self-determined or mandatory meeting attendance, but had simply learned it was easier to find a way to get high if you were around other users and what did it matter that they might be trying to kick? They liked to play the game didn't they or they wouldn't be here alone, right? Thus finding a driver meant hooking up to a guy that had a ride, had a little money in his pocket or in the nearest ATM, and hopefully, a regular place to live that could provide a layover with food on the table for some amount of time until the money ran out or she ran off with the dope and the money too, or the guy decided he really did want to get off the hamster wheel of addiction, recovery, relapse, repeat – ad infinite.

Maybe because both I and one of my early sponsors had been burned in recovery attempts by both types and found an easy road to relapse wasn't so clearly marked but should be avoided at all costs, did my little intellectual pursuit to identify the dangerous ones fascinate me so intently. But most importantly above all, I am serious in my desire to help others in recovery, and if by using my experience and skillful observation to ferret out the danger and threat posed to the unsuspecting, I needed to defend those I can.

I don't want to appear the reformed altruistic do-gooder out to save the innocent children or an avenging angel searching out the Hustlers and Cruisers to punish them. I am not covertly masking a dark egotistical personality avidly searching for some means to act out against the injustices, real or imagined that I and my sponsor were subjected to. Not because I got clean and went straight and I am working out my repressed needs for power or lusting to dominate someone or anyone do as I do. My desire to help those that don't have to experience all that I or my sponsor did, is only a practical and pragmatic concern to take action that the unwise be protected by those who can defend them as they make their way through recovery. It is by no means a Sunday stroll through the park for any of us.

Recovery is rather a scary journey where trusting the wrong person, especially in a room where you can be so easily misled believing everyone is there for the same reasons to get recovered, and that is a dangerous proposition for any male or female. In an ideal world, the rooms can be a safe place to share with and learn from others trying to keep on the straight and narrow one day, one meeting at a time. More critically, meetings necessarily are a place where vulnerabilities are exposed and in the wide open to a large degree, and motives of anyone there aren't, can't, and will never be made certain. We go there if we have a little common sense knowing we are likely surrounded by people who have engaged in every form of deceit and deception there is to support a cruel demanding habit, the biggest being deceiving themselves or they wouldn't be there in the first place. Being even-handed in my appraisal it is also likely some of them or us I like to wryly believe, is worthy of sainthood. Yet still, we were addicted to something and in a room, there is a fifty-fifty chance you engage with someone who is equally vulnerable and is at best left to decipher for yourself who to think about trusting and who you should not trust at all. Sadly self-preservation must be first and foremost your guarded path.

And just when you thought it was safe to get back in the water again you discover another less obvious potential menace... Hormones!

I don't want to seem cynical or lurid about such a sensitive and private matter, but most anyone who has ever been to a smoky room of males and females a time or two can tell you human hormones add a certain unpredictable dimension to recovery. Oh, my... the subtle and covert intrigue I have witnessed when healthy assertive males encounter vulnerable insecure females... neither always wanting to be alone nor feel they can make this journey to recovery by themselves. It is a reality of our times the largest number of people in recovery are thrust together in a place not really an optimum choice to be together, basically isolated from stable relationships with fully predictable futures. Uncertainty abounds and does not make for a rational well thought out decision-making about who is sitting next to you or across the room or who you might feel attracted to. As the numbers for both males and females battling addiction increases so too do the often fragile and uncertain environments of their meeting places outside the better-managed clinical treatment settings.

Many who have chosen to end their addictions don't have the benefit of costly full-time structured treatment with well-trained professionals. Even the availability of general public accessible clinics and centers specializing in recovery treatment are working at overcapacity and it's no secret that they have limited influence in determining who is talking to who about what they do in their private lives.

Without any wry humor applied to illuminate the plight of recovering from substance addiction, and maintaining control over the strong urges that can be insistent and intense until they are fully either satisfied or mastered, the substance addiction might accurately be described as easier to subdue than the normal hormonal addiction men and women naturally share. I offer with honest sympathy the plight some of them share at what is likely one, if not the most, vulnerable time in their lives. Yes, I am fully aware that some sage old clinicians say these settings provide the optimum environment for men and women with similar problems and similar attributes to find practical solutions to similar needs. Yes, I believe that can be true for some and maybe even many but for one small truth... the array of boyfriends and girlfriends, parents and sponsors, and the like waiting at home, or coming to pick them up after the meeting, and the likelihood that two old bad habits can necessarily produce a stable non-substance dependant relationship... for very long... if at all. There are just too many factors that make the smoky rooms without intelligent supervision less than ideal. Hopefully, there will be in the foreseeable future those with real-world understanding about limited interpersonal relationship choices some in recovery have. Social insight and more open and honest perception of the exponentially expanding reality of addiction as a permanent part of our society and how to make it better are necessary.

The social-democratic fabric of modern medicine has got to advance beyond largely organic disease treatment and integrate the growing aspect of substance abuse RECOVERY as part of mainstream medicine with funds necessary to address the issues. It is only getting worse and the social and financial consequences of ignorance are astronomically high when you factor in the total impact on individuals, families, and the institutions that are affected by addiction and the consequent recovery that must follow.

I have revealed something of myself as I have become today aware and observant and concerned with the plight of recovery of so many functioning largely alone, stigmatized, and isolated in small groups. In my first few years of recovery, I learned the differences between being an addict in recovery and being in recovery with other addicts. A sense of responsibility grew steadily as the number of meetings I attended increased and I played a very active role in reaching out to others because I had gone and come back from where they could be going. For the most part, I was successful when I reached out to someone and offered friendship or experience to help make their journey less an unknown struggle and more of a predictable and manageable plan of success. Indeed I made a few notes along the way and don't have to rely on memory alone to illuminate a few of the memorable events marking my passage through more than two dozen smoky rooms. For a couple of years, I had searched out a variety of different meeting groups looking to see if one could offer something others didn't. Most of the different venues were by choice but some by default when stresses about progress on my life plan schedule blew me up emotionally and I needed to go to the closest room I could find to chill. When it was by choice and planning I was searching to know if there were different ways of doing the Steps or talking about them, or even if I did know the right way if there was such a thing. I discovered beyond that most folks in the rooms were addicted to something at some time in their lives, a mix of people from different walks of life who shared valuable and applicable insights I hadn't yet acquired.

One of my room choices stands out and heavily influenced my thinking about being more persistent in getting those in visible distress to trust me. A young girl I met in the waiting room at the Sheltering Arms Recovery Clinic where both she and I were there to see different psychiatrists, shared a little about her favorite room. Rita Morales's glowing descriptions about the Lighthouse Church Friday meetings piqued my interest enough that I asked for the address and the meeting time and I decided I would go for a visit and see for myself. The Lighthouse was only a twenty-minute drive from my house and she said it was a nice group of about twenty friendly people that laughed a lot and they had good refreshments. I thanked her when she got up to see the doc telling her I hoped we would meet there some Friday. Every other Friday for me was a scheduled dinner with my daughter Crystal and her kids and the Fridays between a meeting closest to my house or Kurt's work. I was surprised by my sixth trip to the Lighthouse I was yet to see Rita but remembering that she had told me she was a single mom again, assuming she might have met a guy and was out enjoying a date.

I had intentionally befriended a couple of people at the Lighthouse that were old-timers by my standards, one guy had five years and a couple of women close to my age had four years each. There were a mixed group of guys and gals that had three-plus and I was proudly among them having made the four-year mark a few weeks ago. The balance of a dozen regulars was from one to three years not including two recent newbie's a month out of detox. By now I was confident I would never use again but the meetings were still the most important part of my recovery discipline. Being in this group I learned why some Steps were so much more important than others, and through a combination of sad and some really hilarious recounts of events by the old-timers, why you didn't break the rules of recovery, and what happened when you did.

Addiction is cunning, patient, and for some lethal and fatal. This was not anything I didn't already know but it was good to hear like everyone else what I keep as my second commandment. As my newest sponsor at the Lighthouse repeated before you let your guard down and before you retest any old situations or people, or go visit those places that still give you chills, stop and think it through with the expectation nothing is the same when you are sober.

Not the people but certainly the old hides and haunts were the worst for me. Going anywhere near that part of town I spent so much street time in, even miles out on the interstate driving through that county still makes my stomach churn in pain, like a knife digging in right up under my twice-broken ribs as a grim reminder. I attest to their warnings, being even in the vicinity where any of the numerous overdosed seizures occurred would make me physically sick desperately repressing the sudden urge to vomit. Powerful and extreme they would overwhelm my senses when I allowed anything at all to trigger the hazy vestiges of memory still stuck somewhere in my mind. When I was forced to drive downtown once for a therapy session I desperately needed I had to drive right past the jail I had been in multiple times. It forced up some reminders I try hard to erase. I shared with the Lighthouse group how thankful I was now but not then when the cops busted me with so little probable cause in the wintertime except I was out on the street hustling in freezing ass cold weather, no clients insight, and the cops who knew me were afraid I'd die in some alley or in a dumpster like poor Jessica that she had been left in after an overdose and the john didn't want to be charged in her death or tied to it in any way. They would grab me up put me in a warm cell and feed me two meals a day and release me uncharged when the cold streak passed. I give unguarded praise always to those men of honor whose duty was to enforce the law which they did, but I know so much better today loving compassion and empathy was extended for my care and well being compelling each one of them to GIVE of themselves as they did. How few men today never having worn a uniform or a badge will rise to that level of morality and humanity to do equally? Very few even think at that level let alone act. It is I believe as the Lord says "I came for the sinners, not the saved." It is through the noble selfless acts of the Kurt's, the Joe's, and the Merle's and their kind we receive the Lord's divine mercy so generously.

 I saw at the Lighthouse one gal, Suzanne, who I knew was hooking and I was certain she was still headed down that addiction path and I felt her misery. At all six meetings, I had attended she was there and looking more ragged around the edges every time. I was far from the perceptive observer I would yet become, and I lacked the needed skills to get past her aloofness both times I tried. I saw her one final time at my seventh visit there and it was really clear to me and everyone she hadn't tripped and fallen as she claimed when someone attempted to console her for her unfortunate injuries, somebody had beat on her a bit. She flat-out coolly rejected anyone who tried to approach her. She went so far to say she was going to move away to some other group if everybody didn't just leave her alone. Wow, it was a shock to all of us. I stopped going to the Lighthouse after nine meetings never seeing Rita there but made a few casual phone friends who I called and we three met for coffee once and had a good afternoon. I have a sad memory about the Lighthouse because the one girl Becky I had coffee with called me one Saturday morning two weeks later to tell me she had heard in the meeting the night before that Suzanne had died. The police had contacted the group sponsor looking for information on her and asked a lot of questions, but that's all anyone knew or was told, apparently, she had a group newsletter and phone numbers on it in her bag. I felt really bad that I could not break through the same defenses that once held me in bondage to reach her and help her avoid the ultimate tragedy that ended any hope of recovering her dreams. Perhaps meeting Rita was my Guide leading me to the Lighthouse to discover through the tragedy of Suzanne, I still needed better skills and determination to learn them.

Support is something we all need.

An addict in recovery or straight, never used, CEO leading the troops to victory, there must be someone or a lot of someone's helping you get to the top or stay there. For souls like me and the thousands more across the map who march every morning into the valley of the shadow of death, we need someone leading us, walking beside us or following closely behind us, or all of these. Our sense of purpose and sense of self needs steady assurance that we are not alone. It's in our DNA. For some, it's often enough to believe there is God or the Holy Ghost walking right there with them, and some need that and more. We can find a lot of those in the pulpits of the church, the loners in the laboratories peering into a microscope to find cures to save us all, or on the side of Mt. Everest inching to that near-sacred peak in search of their destiny. But with little doubt the preacher knows the masses will be in attendance on Sunday, the not really mad scientists know peers are looking over their shoulders from every direction, and arriving at the peak the mountain climber knows many are attached to the rope trailing behind him and millions of eyes are looking in anticipation from around the world as the victory flag is thrust into the cold white snow.

Is there anyone really who doesn't need and want somebody to validate their purposed struggle and achievements thereof? Is there anyone who does not need and want someone to acknowledge and validate their worth as individuals making contributions to family, friends, in the workplace, or as a member of society? I think we can all agree on the premise we all need someone. In the recovery meeting places everywhere the positive implicit agreement that keeps everyone coming is they are coming to support and be supported on the common journey maintaining sobriety.

My own need for support was still there even when I felt I hardly needed any. I had Kurt for my first shaky steps out of jail, I had my children, I had several available sponsors, and I had the handful of new casual friends made in the rooms. They were there supporting me. And I, them. I finally had a couple of adult female friends to talk about life with that I had not had since grade school. I was eagerly looking forward now about six years into my recovery to developing friends in the workplace when my health and my lingering criminal record made it possible. I was growing intellectually curious to know if I could be a friend and have normal friends who had never abused alcohol or drugs or submitted themselves to the ugly of that world. There were the still critical and unavoidable elements I could easily overlook on all the mostly good days I was having, the lingering unconscious, psychological, and biophysical effects of the long dependent use of cocaine. Yes indeed, how much I wanted to believe I and my doctors and supporters in the rooms waved a magic wand and I would never be bothered by the not erasable never to punish me again... memories of those madly euphoric everything is okay and I can change the world... cocaine highs. Yep, they were still too fresh in my mind-body paradigm even after six tough but good years of detox, prayer, inpatient treatment, out-patient treatment, cold showers, pacing the room, long walks, and yes attending these meetings in smoky rooms... talking gallantly and nobly about how long I have been sober... not using DRUGS!

Here is the paradox each one of us faces there.

You are close quarters in a room with maybe a dozen or even two other formerly addicted souls... and whether you like it or not you are still talking indirectly about your favorite DRUGS! Yes indeed the explicit and implicit topics are about Recovering from your drug addiction, but the harsher psychological biological neurological reality is each of us must stimulate once, twice, or who knows how many times in a meeting, that part of the brain where our memories about the DRUGS we probably enjoyed immensely the first time or how many times we used them??? Oh... that's just the tip of the iceberg really! You have walked with me through a few of these smoky room adventures and you have likely come to the same conclusion I ultimately did after eight years, smoky rooms ain't always the best or most conducive environments as they are proffered to be for kicking the DRUG habit and fully engaging sobriety.

But what is true is this: It is the Individuals themselves that take seriously their efforts to help others that make the important differences. There were a half dozen just like myself I met over the years who didn't need the smoky rooms for themselves; no, they go back time and again to push, pull or shove someone else out of the trap and off the hamster wheel and show them how to Engage The Solution to Recovery.

Indeed it is a dilemma and a paradox and maybe you are beginning to understand two things. One, why so many well-intentioned ideas about how to get to that drug-free state of consciousness are not really working out like so many expected they should, and two, the most important part, why so... so... so... many addicts relapse... over and over again.

There are some changes needed, not in the AA or NA basic plan, that's fine, but it's the HOW you conduct that business of recovery room meetings, and the WHO leads them with WHAT training that needs to be addressed ASAP.

I sincerely hope those changes can happen and happen soon.

10

Spirituality

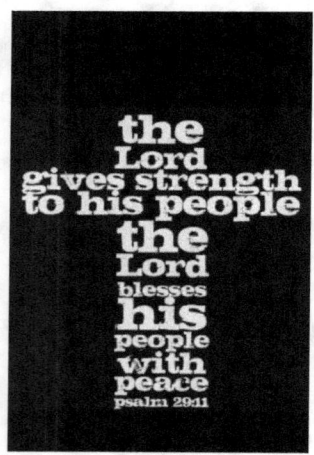

The Lord was asking for complete surrender to His 'will' and with what willful determination I possessed, I surrendered. He gave me a choice to trust Him or trust in the world, the same world of darkness and confusion that was my life for most of it. I made the choice to let go of my way and accept His. I accepted Sister Ann's intercession for me to say Hi, and my first "Yes Ma'am" gave authority to her as the Lord's servant to guide me on my journey to salvation. It was my small degree of trust, indeed all I had within me that was magnified sufficiently to my needs on that first day in her care to begin the long process of healing that was ahead of me. I had taken the first fateful unsure step into the Kingdom of our Lord and joined to others as a Warrior for truth and that truth set me free from all that lay behind me in ruins and destruction of myself. My flesh nature was replaced with a foundation of Spiritual truth and obedience to strengthen me and guide my footsteps on my true path the Lord would make straight to carry me through the narrow gate of eternal life.

"Your will Lord, not mine be done," I spoke aloud in the early morning in my first day of freedom. I felt that small tingle I would know again and again telling me there was something alive and knowing within me that it was not my own but something given. I was in a small cell but it was not a prison any longer. It was a place of rest and solitude to restore me and give me safety and peace that I had not known before. I was given refuge and quiet to study the Scriptures and learn of another realm of experience that was above what I had lived in the world. My eyes were opening to what was beyond me in the empty daily toils that had given me nothing real to sustain me. I saw for myself where my will, my purpose in living, was vain and bereft of any real value and my life had been without purpose above an existing hour to hour day to day stumbling in darkness with an unmerciful emptiness inside of me.

I was seeing there was a will that was greater and stronger than my own and it had a purpose it had meaning and it was the truth in action. It was the will of God and I began each day when I awoke to embrace my true purpose and that purpose was to know God and to love Him with all of my heart my mind my body and my soul. For it was in that place, that once small place, that was each hour growing as I came to know a loving and merciful God that was my soul. It was that very essence of God that had taken dominion over all of those other things that was my soul – my soul was the sum of my heart my mind and my body and was the completeness of who I was within God and in the Kingdom.

I accepted as my truth in those long days and nights of study and learning when I surrendered. I opened the gateway to my soul, and though small now, yet it could only grow if I chose to remain submissive to His will each day as Sister Ann guided my discoveries of who I was becoming. I knew little but I knew more each day and each day offered something important and meaningful. Every question in my mind that I sought answers for received not an answer from her but indeed often another question pushing me to look ever deeper within the word and within myself to find meaning. In time I would understand and embrace that meaning might be unique to every person and meant for illumination for the needs of the one and not always for the many. It was with that insight gained in prayer I prayed to go in the way of understanding that I was finding as a soul free'd from the delusions in mind and body that drugs and hardships that was my flesh way. I was learning and beginning to live the truth of the relationship with God was a personal relationship. There were not many Gods … but there are many truths and we must each search out that truth for ourselves that we come to know the glory of God in our own unique lives of experience.

My daily journey was both frightening and exciting. Always there was the new replacing the old daily ways of thinking and existing in turmoil on the street gave way to a more peaceful regimen and structure and a balance too of being a normal person not hustling to feed my body and addiction. Within the confines of law and order, organization and routine, and the morality of normal everyday people, in my new refuge of hope, I was undoing the harsh emotional hopelessness that governed the only choices I had on the street and unleashing the power of hope. I was challenged each day to take authority over my future with knowledge and understanding laid before me using patience and reflection to assemble the pieces of the puzzle life would be when I left the safe harbor I was in.

I was petrified some days when new perceptions took hold and I knew how much was lost of me and my abilities to lead a normal life following rules and expectations of people over who I had little or no control. Just where was I to fit when I was set free to make my own way again? I would have to carry with me very soon the long list of mistakes I had made before to be presented to those with strict codes of right and wrong to accept or reject me as one of them? Yes, indeed there were real reasons to be fearful and apprehensive when I got out there... and now I clearly see so well why relapse time and again was the result of being overwhelmed by the enormity of it all. Yet here I sat under Sister Ann's knowing gaze with a worksheet in hand breaking it all down with a simple little plan to try once again to make my ascent to the top. But she assured me, and so did the Lord we shared, I was not anymore that weak frightened woman fragile and alone who must climb a tall jagged mountain to see the light, for now, I had powerful strength and vision to see it was not a mountain at all but only a little hill.

When I talked to people inside my temporary study hall, the jailers and guards, and all those who worked inside administering the day-to-day functions, they were not all sympathetic to me and my presence at first. Why should they be? Many had seen me before some once some multiple times, and a couple hadn't seen me until now but had seen others just like me and they had little reason to act towards me but as their jobs and duties required of them. What did they see and hear? When I arrived I was a little ragged around the edges and had acquired a stand back and leave me alone demeanor from the street. I wore it well and made it clear with looks and body language you didn't want to mess with me unless I tell you to and if you violated that non-verbal message I was going to hurt you if I could. Yeah, that was me! The domineering little self-assured gal who carried a very sharp razor knife barely out of sight in her bra almost all the time was tough!

Of course, it wasn't how I really felt or thought, not at all. It was an act I had learned the first few weeks on the street to throw at you because I was actually scared to death of my own shadow and my plan, which I had to follow many a time, was run like hell if it looked like there was going to be any kind of conflict beyond anyone just being a little pissed off at me and mumbling under their breath the extent of any aggression towards me. And truly lots of people who knew me said I was a very great actress and said it probably kept me out of trouble more times than I wanted to know. So that was the me that most everyone but Sister Ann and Sister Doris saw when they booked me in. Yeah, I was tough as nails... trembling inside but keeping up the act in simple self-defense against I didn't know what that could happen being here a year as I thought I would be.

On day two I let my guard down a little and after two weeks I was just the person I was, shy and timid. Scared and sad about being here a year but knowing it was way better than out there working the streets to stay high, I tried to find some solace in being clean finally, even if it was only for a few weeks. In those two weeks, I saw they changed a little as my act diminished and there was a lot more compassion in there than I was expecting. After Sister Ann accepted me into her program again, what an immediate change they saw! I can say honestly that the more dignified and courteous I acted toward them, most of them returned it with ease. Surprisingly I discovered quickly the majority don't like locking you up and guarding you but the reality is they do their best to treat the non-hardened criminal type that hasn't committed violence against others with quite a bit of civil respect and I think it's by choice. The simple truth is they have spirits too for the most part and they treat you as you treat them.

When I told Sister Doris one day about details of my past and how long I had been on the street she asked me very straightforward, how I had survived so long doing what I was doing and was in as good of shape as I appeared. I was a little bit surprised by the way she asked the question having no knowledge of where the question was leading. But the words out of my mouth surprised her just as much because I spoke it so quickly and so automatically and so honestly and her body language indicated it was not at all what she was expecting to hear from me. My answer was, "God. And I read my Bible every day."

I believe what she expected to hear was a hardened answer equivalent to I was tough and smart and didn't let anyone mess with me. I had heard the same kind of thinking from so many gals on the street who actually had come from tough as hell backgrounds and had taken their fair share of abuse from their pimps and the violent tricks they often encountered when they hit the streets. If you weren't already hardcore when you arrived to do the street life of hooking and drugging you either got tough or you were left with one choice to survive — Get Off The Street! Only choices you had to avoid a fatal OD or a fatal trick. Too many, and a couple of them unfortunately I knew, weren't tough, didn't get tough, didn't leave soon enough, and ended up at the morgue or disappeared forever. That was the cost of being out there.

Sister Doris stared at me for a long, long minute looking me right in the eyes and I held her gaze, not defiantly or personally, but truly I was that certain of the power that God was holding over my life out there it just came out very strong and unwavering. She would only months later reveal the effect my response had, that it predetermined the basis of how she would interact with me and where she needed to start in her role as my spiritual guide. I learned that she had exchanged with Sister Ann, a very intriguing insight into what she thought was my weakness, namely it was not whether or not I believed in God and believed in the sin of what I had been doing, it was her belief that I simply lacked knowledge of how God worked and how much power He had in our lives if we submitted ourselves to him.

Sister Ann revealed what Sister Doris told her only when I was a week away from completing all the course work and had received the extent of their combined guidance that it was why the relationship they both had with me was so different from that with other gals in the program. I was vaguely aware of it a few times but when she explained a little more about what they expected for my future I was totally stunned. They were anticipating I would go into the Convent if I could given what they had observed and heard in the beginning and the unique way I would reveal I perceived God, which to them was the basic precepts of Nuns... yet, I was a —hooker— or had been. She made a final comment about Mary Magdalene that remains a secret within me, but her words very heavily guided ALL of my spiritual growth from that day forward. At a very early age, I believed I could someday be a Nun but that was before words were spoken within my family and the awful thing happened with Pete that left me in dark shame so deep I felt there was no way I was acceptable anymore to God to be a Nun.

The structure of my time, offered ample time to be with others and I did engage with other gals who believed themselves in jail, but it was my true nature and quest to spend all time that allowed me to exist within my refuge and safe harbor in solitude. My answer to their confusing question, "Why do you spend so much time in your cell girl?" was "I am studying." It could go from there with twenty questions largely revolving around what could I possibly be studying that being in a 'Cell' was so good. And of course, there was the occasional insinuation about sexual things I simply laughed off no matter how crudely they were implied. I was in a different realm now and it was at times difficult not to be in study or prayer or in meditative reflective thought, which my most beloved Pastor calls 'supplication' and says that's what I am doing. To those not familiar with Hebrew or Greek doctrine it is best described as prayer with a purpose, an explicit purpose seeking counsel with God for something or about something that is for the person praying, as opposed to praying for others or being in prayer perhaps about the general well being of many or the world.

Supplication to God, or more precisely for me, from me to the Holy Ghost, is like the petition that I started writing to a Judge for an early release... that was ultimately granted. In my Petition to the Judge, I stated what I was asking him for, why I was asking, and why I believed the early release I was petitioning for should be granted. I had done my homework on the legal premises with what was available to me, the Florida Statutes that governed my incarceration based on the charges that were against me, and the Judges legal authority to make decisions for or against my Petition. In simplest terms I knew what he could rule on and the way he could rule and the limits of his authority. So in the very same manner, supplication is the same. It requires that you read the Bible a little or a lot based on just what you think you need and are on the same page so to speak with the Lord. You have to know what the rules are based on precedent, earlier law, and rulings on precise applications historically, and you have to know on what authority the Lord can rule or act on. So boiling it down a little more you need to read the Old Testament deemed the law of God to identify what the law says about what you are asking for, read the New Testament to find out what Jesus the Son of God had to say on the matter, determine identifying specific parables or 'instructions' on which Jesus made, not law but more so mercy and grace, and if you are pretty sure you are right about what you are asking for and can cite the specific criteria as a precedent from His instructions, then you ask for a ruling on it —EXPECTING TO RECEIVE THE RULING OR THE THING—and believe and act or behave as if it's already been granted in your favor. And then be patient and observe and listen for further instructions received in prayer if necessary and do as you will with the Lord's blessings. It's really not so hard if you practice a little or maybe a lot, it does sometimes require a little patience depending on what you are asking for because there are a lot of moving parts in the world and in the Kingdom. Oh, I left out a little something... that part about saying and believing and acting on —Your Will Lord Not My Own. That's kind of important because it just won't usually work to ask the Lord to make elephants fly. However, if you are very careful with your choice of words, such as not asking the Lord to give elephants WINGS to fly with, you can just proceed down to the airport after your supplication is granted because he likely will make you aware there is a 747 landing at the airport this afternoon called the Elephant Express.

So... that's what supplication is and that's pretty much how it works. I haven't ever asked for elephants getting advanced mobility but I have asked for forgiveness of my sins and a few other things and I got out of jail serving only half the mandatory sentence a different judge imposed and I did a short time later received a requested very special friend I needed when I was standing in the freezing cold at midnight with nobody, no money, no place to go, and no way to get there... and my requested friend brought me dinner too because the Lord knew I was hungry and I hadn't even put that in the supplication. So I continue to pray daily and to practice supplication when I need something special and I have learned much more about how God and Jesus and the Holy Ghost all work together, which was the very thing Sister Ann and Sister Doris said was insufficient in me. So I corrected that and make more corrections each and every day.

The Judge set me free early and the Deputy opened the exit door out of my refuge safe harbor (Jail) and away I went thankful that I had some very compassionate people, and a wonderful pair of devout Nuns with a heck of a lot of street smarts and an eye for detail, guiding me back into a treacherous world I was better prepared to engage than I ever was before. I felt a little sad I had to leave... it was that good for me because I had formed a deep personal bond to the degree I could with the Sisters. In my mind was a certain sadness that some or all of the others who had originally had the good fortune to be admitted to the Sisters program didn't finish or weren't leaving early as I was. In my heart, I wanted for them to find their Spiritual truth and embrace a positive set of choices and find a deep and lasting relationship with the Lord that can fulfill their every need.

The challenge to finding your own Spiritual truth is that we live in a largely secular world, meaning we are bombarded through every form of media about 'material things' and their acquisition being the road to happiness. Heck, they would have us believe that material things are the superhighway to happiness. Is that true? Is the fine clothes and shoes, the flashy cars, the fancy apartment or house, the two-week vacations in some overpriced tourist trap somewhere, ad infinite your road to happiness and fulfillment? If it is that's fine. If you have all those things already and you are happy, that's fine too. I am glad for you and I truly hope you continue in your prosperity. Personally, though I never had all of those trappings myself I have known way too intimately many who have and all I saw was an insatiable hunger for more and I was part of that hunger and I made them or so they claimed happy for a short time. Never mind all the stuff they talked about why they needed me and a big bag of drugs to get to the next level.

It's ironic to me when I got to know a few of them a lot better how much they talked about being you guessed it, TRAPPED by their wealth. How much deception they had to engage in –which included their wife– how many hours they were forced to work keeping the plates spinning, how many lawyers they had to pay, how many of that – how much of this, all leading to the misery of the drugs they had to do right now with me telling them they were mister superstar. It wasn't to have fun it was to maintain their emotional stability enough to keep engaging the game. How pitiful for both of us and everybody else in their line of fire accumulating more money to buy more things to do the things that they were doing and when they got down from the high, telling me how damn miserable they were and they wished they could just get off the hamster wheel they were on. Well, we did have something in common after all, they were rich, I was a poor working girl and we both hated the hamster wheel we were running at top speed. And we both wanted to get off but couldn't for exactly the same reason. There just wasn't enough yet to be happy and fulfilled. He needed the fun and games and the drugs for momentary relief, and I needed the fun and games for the drugs it would buy me to feed my addiction for temporary relief. Wow!

I found my way off the wheel finally and left any hunger for unneeded material things behind me... forever. I had submitted myself to the deception of more things too easily when I got married and needed fancier clothes that I never had, a little more jewelry than I had need of, a bigger and nicer apartment, fine furniture, two cars and a truck, a nice expensive vacation to a tourist trap put on a high rate credit card, ad infinite. Then my husband who was the hard believer in accumulating wealth and told me I was a fool if I didn't believe we would be happier with all the stuff, and then more stuff, and then more stuff. But we weren't happier. We were working even more hours because we bought a fine new home to put all the stuff in, plus more, then it was taking his check AND my check too from a job I loved to pay the bills, and then he brought home that coke and said, "my dear wife this is the stuff that will make us even happier!" Oh hell. I had never heard of the stuff, and no it didn't make me happy but it sure lost me my career and made me hooked, and what tiny little Spiritual truth I had been able to explore barely out of being a teenager was too little to save me from Spiritual meltdown. There was a God but I certainly didn't pray when I should have and of course, getting high didn't leave any need for a God or prayer it just didn't even seem necessary I was so euphorically happy- as long as there was more and more when I came down. And there you have it. The unreality of more on the superhighway to nowhere you want to go.

As I told Sister Doris it was always somewhere in my mind... my soul in truth—that there was a God. I was tricked by that white fire so badly from the beginning I just stopped believing for a lot of wrong reasons. I was unworthy of saving from hell I think. Maybe I learned from Dr. Pat and somebody in a meeting that I was unconsciously hoping I would die and I kept using and having those seizures secretly hoping me or God was going to simply let me go and it would all be over with. I would be set free. Well, that didn't completely happen but what I will tell you is this. All those stories you hear about near-death experiences... believe the substance of them. Personally, it wasn't near for me, it was absolutely more than once and the EMTs will testify on a Bible, certainly, the one they always found conveniently open somewhere nearby me when they zapped me back to having a pulse again. I don't still have that Bible sadly, wish I did, but I honestly believe it was the major factor. I can't explain exactly how it saved me three, yes three times, and yes there is a white light and you do feel calm and as many have stated was unequivocally true for themselves, I too FELT a presence in that place where we are suspended for a time. That presence in my belief system is the Holy Ghost. Real and tangible for those who go looking because you knock enough times that door will always open revealing a presence guiding you in life and that presence, if you have connected, is absolutely merciful and the keeper of life.

I experienced a true calm within me a peacefulness as I was quietly watching the sun come up on the horizon of the ocean on a very calm day. The water looks like glass and the sun is shimmering off it and reflecting eternal Peace. The warm breeze blew softly over the water touching my face it was like a soft hug from a close friend. I remained there in the warm sand in the early morning reflecting on all the wonderful things that had happened over the time since I changed the course and direction of my life.

I do not know the exact meaning of the vision that soon followed of a dog running down the beach at the water's edge and his owner who I did not recognize was calling to him, I never felt more comfortable in my life as I sat there observing the happy relationship between the two. I knew I could face anything that would come at me. From where I was in this moment it was going forward and beckoning me onward. The emergence of another consciousness hidden away in a realm that was familiar came to share peace and hope with a group of others approaching me from across the horizon. Another warm breeze touched my soul... and I was suddenly returned to the here and now where I was.

My Spiritual journey continues each day with thoughts about the mysteries of my life and mysteries that span the ages back in time. Though I live in the presence of each day my mind is filled with questions and things to reflect upon and things I must know. There are daydreams and there are night dreams but not every day does either come. There are revelations that I see without notice and must turn over in my mind for days and sometimes weeks and some still remain that do not seem to make sense but that is not often. I just catalog those that don't seem to fit because every day I write in one or many journals not relying upon memory only. I do not watch T.V. much at all for lots of good reasons mainly I believe they contaminate so much of my mind and my senses. When I do watch the T.V. it's a science or National Geographic or the BBC explorations of the microcosm of the sea and the forest's floor somewhere I wish I could go. There is much to gain from feeding the mind a steady diet about the mysteries of the heavens and the earth for we are in so many ways interconnected to it all.

Evolution sure, there's lots of good proof but there are some intriguing conundrums that reveal there is something that evolution did not create, and thus God has given man's mind things to explore that he become as promised a master of his domain. Within my own mind, I have assembled great questions about what is out there beyond where the Hubble telescope can take our minds. I ask, can I or anyone really explain what we are seeing or how we know what we do. Some days as I read the books I have been given about God, Jesus, the Spirit, the Holy Ghost, and Angels and miracles, I wonder will we ever know how it all works together? Just how many pieces are there to the puzzle of us and them and all the rest of the stuff we perceive and what we yet can't perceive but what good science tells us is there or here or somewhere?

But just as surely as I ask these questions and make these inquiries of the Spirit, in a short time I receive little prompts from God that kind of answers it all. One day He brings me to ponder and believe it possible I can see what I see and know what I know and it will all make perfect sense why we are here and what is our Divine purpose if there be such a thing? Oh well, time for a nap my mind has tired and I have other inquires to make when I have rested.

The Lord said just listen for my voice and I will lead where you need to go!

Each morning rain or shine begins the same way. Good time spent reading from daily devotionals of inspiration and giving that time to converse with the Lord. Can I have your guidance to walk with me through another good day?

'Yes' He says and I take my first steps, I read I write I journal I ponder all before the work duty calls and off I go to help them one and all.

I spent years learning about the ministry of the Lord, the love of a power greater than myself. It amply rewards and each day is more spiritually significant than the day before and so I continue my path to know and use the gifts of my higher power and I prosper. I know that each day will always offer up new challenges to the smooth road I wanted to have but I know I will always be given a way to make the crooked road straight if that is His will in this one day this week and month till my last breath is taken.

The Light at the end of the proverbial tunnel is just a bit brighter than the last time I looked. Allow yourself the same chance to know and follow God as I have and to know His Word. Jesus came for the Sinner's, not the Saved; He doesn't look down on us other than to watch over us. Hope and Faith are all through the Good Book and it is exactly where I find the strength each day to go forward. To trust in a power greater than myself is to trust that if I walked the path in front of me now it will always be the right road to follow.

Psalms 23 is something I repeat after my prayers each day and something I find powerful to hold my new life and recovery strong. It goes like this:

> The Lord is my Shepard, I shall not want.

> He makes me lie down in green pastures, He leads me beside still waters, He restores my soul.
>
> He guides me in paths of righteousness for His name's sake. Even though I walk through the valley of the shadow of death, I shall fear no Evil,
>
> for you are with me.
>
> Your rod and Your staff they comfort me.
>
> You prepare a table before me in the presence of my enemies. You anoint my head with oil, my cup overflows.
>
> Surely goodness and mercy shall follow me all the days of my life, and I shall dwell in the house of the Lord forever.
>
> Amen.

MY SHADOW OF DEATH WAS TRULY MY ADDICTION AND TODAY MY STILL WATERS ARE MY RECOVERY.

So what will be your turning point?

Where is that critical turning point in your life?

Helping you to see the new you hiding in there? Pick up a Bible and feel its power, you might be surprised by the changes in your life. I know believing in a God for some is beyond their credulity; how could a loving God allow so much bad to happen in the world? Believe and remember that good and evil exist for us to be able to choose the course we want as individuals and deal with the consequences of our choices, that is how we are closer or farther away from God.

We are born right in the middle of the ruler where it is six inches the one way and six inches to the other. At one end is pure evil and at the other pure perfection. I have journeyed both ways multiple times but as I have sought God and the Spirit of truth, my truth is always moving towards me from pure perfection. Yet I do not ever ignore so too is the Evil of this world always moving from that other end in my direction, but it is by my choice to always be aware and remain as best as I humanly can moving away from Evil and thus I proceed through each day in the light and always in my Spirituality seeking Gods loving protection keeping evil from passing across the centerline towards me.

11

A Rising Star...

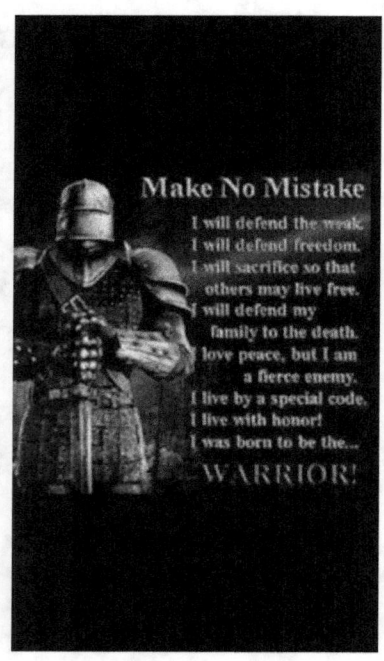

Yes, indeed my prayers were heard... kind of like usual now.

Humble I was and I had actually learned a little patience too that kind of made it all work. The Lord revealed step by step how I was walking the path He had chosen for me. As it says, "Your Will Not My Own" was the way I got there, or here, whichever it was. I was receiving little prompts now and then that made me smile when the out of nowhere image or images appeared in my mind with something distinct that over a few years I learned to perceive the connection being made. I guess a psychologist would call it insight, I think Dr. Pat might have told me that's what they were. Oh my, did I ever need them sometimes too? I almost couldn't survive without them. "Thank you, Lord, for this day!" I said out loud. I think I am going to get my own place and be that independent woman I had planned to be for oh so long!

I had just returned from a steady brisk one-mile walk taking in as much of the cool February morning air as I could feeling ever more thankful my stamina had increased to do it with ease early in the morning. The knee injury that kept me on crutches for over six months had slowly healed and though I would always have a perceptible posture imbalance, over a year of steady effort I had gotten to this level defeating the surgeons and the physical rehab therapist's prognostications I likely could never endure that much continuous stress on it. Never mind the excruciating pain those first few months of tearful one trip around the block in one hour and then two or three hours of ice packs. I remember lots of walks before the injury in the first weeks and months and yes a full year keeping the stresses and the jitters leftover from my long addiction under control. Relapse happens long before the addicted mind and body drinks, smokes, snorts, or shoots, that relapse is always one very bad choice away. I had pushed myself to walk almost every day to keep my mind and body engaged in things to defeat the subtle, and then the overt, stimulus to use if I let it advance that far. I heard a guy in an early meeting say something that humorously stuck with me, "You got to get there first. You got to be always ahead of it!"

Indeed I learned quickly how true that was when I put off doing something to avoid too much quiet still time in that first year. If I wasn't sleeping I was busy and after those first couple of months, I was just simply too tired to be awoken in the middle of the night with mental urges or worst yet, images of the routine to get high. Were they ever their own kind of trip sometimes too! It was like having a crazy nightmare while you were wide awake. But it became pretty clear to me early that meetings and people in recovery were necessary to structure my time and fill my life. I learned my lesson well from repeated relapses where that old road would always lead me back to. But today, a clear head and growing confidence from the challenges I had met and the successes I had achieved, was beckoning me forward and up to the next level. My own internal voice was cheering me on with some positive gains, "you have many years clean, a little money saved, and the chance to be comfortable working smart every day and looking out in front of you to a stable and happy future." I knew there were some limits to what I could do, but I was steady engaging the right attitude and taking care of my mind and body with diet and exercise, and always pushing myself to discover just what those limits really were.

I heard it said in a meeting by someone that real success comes when we replace bad habits with good habits. I took that seriously and remained mindful of that until I was past the point of no return to bad habits because my time and my life were filled to near capacity with basically all new things. Both my first and second relapses occurred because I repeated bad habits, or more simply, I went back to hang out with friends in neighborhoods where drugs were a way of life. There was hardly a house in a pretty big section in that part of town I called my turf that you couldn't score drugs of almost any kind day or night. I simply just didn't go back there now and I wondered too were any of those I called friends were really that. Maybe the cops actually were my real friends after all, but I didn't think so then and I actually have called a couple of them and thanked them... and asked them if I could interview them if I ever wrote a book. They mostly laughed but said come talk about it... if I ever wrote a book.

Wow. You just never know how some things come around!

I actually had made some progress with new habits before I relapsed those previous times. The things that worked before on those recovery tries were involvement at daily meetings, hanging out with recovery friends and acquaintances, and occasionally making plans with them to hang out at the park or coffee house afterward and sharing what we were doing to rebuild our lives. We were usually in agreement about believing we could not just go to say 'hello' and not get high. This never happens because if you had for even a day been thinking about it, chances are pretty good you're already in full-blown relapse and just didn't know it yet.

I was frightened just a bit of the change I was about to implement in my life. I decided to take Auntie Hazel up on her offer to come out to Texas for a visit and called her. I dialed her up and when the phone rang I felt a wave of anxiety race through me and I felt like I had been struck by lightning when she said "Hello." I burst out into tears and with a sobbing voice asked if I could come and see her. It took a long minute maybe more for her to calm me down enough to understand what I was saying. When her soothing voice had brought me out of the confusion I told her in some fashion that Kurt and I were splitting up. She assured me everything was going to work out but she was very sure she was looking forward to me coming to see her. She was certain we would have a wonderful time.

I was relieved I had someone to share the uncertainty I was feeling about the transition. I was feeling what any female would when a relationship ends and it was compounded by the mental conflict created by both wanting to be on my own and giving up the security in a relationship. Aunt Hazel was adamant that she get me a plane ticket herself and that I should come as soon as I could. I packed a few things in a suitcase after talking with her, spent the night tossing and turning in bed with conflicts from the present and a host from the past, got up and paced a few hours, and off that afternoon I went to Texas.

It was a short flight and I was very excited when I landed to be back under better circumstances to my old hometown. They were indeed glad to see me as I was glad to see all of them. Aunt Hazel's hugs were still as comforting as they were so many years ago. It was a genuine family reunion with Auntie and my cousins Bella and Ali. My cousins were not much more than babies when I left Texas for Florida and it was good to see they had matured into fine women that were the epitome of the girl next door so often written about. We did a lot of fun things, visiting a lot of landmarks around San Antonio and went to the Alamo and I was surprised to see it was not as big as it appeared to be in so many movies. It was a busy town and had a lot of tourism and there was plenty to see and do, we just didn't have the time for but I thought I would one day go back and visit again.

There were a few difficult moments talking about the ups and downs of my life and why things happened as they did. They had found out about Pete not too many years ago and were very sad that it happened to me and saw pretty clearly it may have been something that was the cause of so much destruction I went through years later. They were women too and understood how our trust and our perception of relationships were subject to pretty harsh realities sometimes and we didn't recover so easily. But it was good for me to share the truth as I knew it so that there were not always those misgivings in my head about how the folks back home thought of me. There was a new bond of love and compassion formed between us that I will always hold dear. Going back home to clear my name so to speak was the right thing to do so I could move forward with my life. I left there knowing my future was not as frightening as I thought it to be and I was stronger when I left than when I arrived.

Seeing the big place I called home now from the air as we made the final approach into Palm Beach Airport was a good thing. It didn't scare me anymore from way up here as it had on the ground for so many years. It just didn't look that hard to navigate anymore and I could see there was a lot of ways out of town if it were ever to come to that good or bad. I hit the ground running and Kurt was still the gentleman of honor he was when I met him. He helped me pack up and move to my new place. Wow! How long it had taken was not that few weeks I foresaw it being when I got out of jail to finally get here. Oh how much we learn as we get a little older and a little more perceptive about the limits in our lives.

There were lots of adjustments to make moving from the comfort zone Kurt and I had created for a time into a new zone full of choices and decisions that I thought I had all foreseen. Oh Well... every day was a learning experience for a while. Rude landlords, cars breaking down, bills to pay, things that I couldn't do that I wanted to do for one reason or another. There were days of frustration because I was simply trying to do too much too soon for all the wrong reasons. No one seemed to be able to move as fast as I did and the simple reality was I had become a highly disciplined person and expected the rest of the world to move at my pace. Oh well... I learned to adjust one day at a time. But I stayed focused and I read my Bible every morning and prayed and I made every day count.

And the day finally came... I had a new job. A thrift store! Yep, here I was back on that time clock just like pretty much everyone else. It felt scary but it was also very comforting, I was going to continue my journey to being a respectable member of society again. And hey it's no secret I should keep now, I had fears that someone would recognize me from my old life. Even though one part of me was saying it won't happen here another part just kept telling me not to be so sure. Little anxiety to get the day going the Lord was whispering in my ear and use it wisely if you don't mind, please.

Employable. Responsible. Dependable. Loveable. Happy... ME!

Believing after a few weeks on the job smiling, greeting people saying you are welcome a lot, and all the good things that go with being around a lot of new people every day, I felt I was ready to start on some personal relationships beyond my recovery friends. I got on the old computer to join the online world of dating. I found a guy named Mark who seemed to like my profile and his was okay too, so we met up for dinner. Well, that wasn't that difficult because the two of us hit it off quite well. We enjoyed our time together as platonic friends going to NASCAR racing events, weekly dinner out, the beach watching the waves roll in and out, the whole gamut of dating... without the sex part of course. I really wanted someone I could develop a long-term relationship with but for me it needed to be just that, taking the time required to see if it was a good fit... before sex blew it all up and became all the wrong things I didn't want. Mark, on the other hand, was more committed from the third date to being a couple and make it as a couple permanently than I was ready for.

I had not even thought about dating anyone for six months after leaving Kurt. But nonetheless, we became very good friends... without the sex... and I enjoy all the things we do together as does he. So indeed my prayers for that friend were answered. I had fully accepted I was probably still a good ways from being ready to have any kind of intimate relationship because I had learned through my female friendships with non-recovery gals there was a hell of a lot I did not understand about men and intimacy having been in abusive relationships and nothing more. The Lord agreed so I stuck to the limits that felt right for now.

I did go on a few other dates because being a female I think it's always in our mind somewhere to have a mate or be a mate. I didn't find Mr. Right of course but I did enjoy a lot of good lunches and dinners and a few strolls on the beach trying to connect in the right way but it just wasn't meant to happen. And there was that little nagging from the Lord telling me, my judgment, probably needed a little more time to improve in the Prince Charming search.

But I need to be honest about something else, namely, the online dating thing poses lots of dangers to the unwary or unwise.

I agreed to meet a guy I met on Date.com at his beach house for dinner to get to know each other and have a nice evening. What transpired was far from that because while I was sipping my iced tea I started feeling dizzy, which I didn't understand at first, until my instincts told me I had been drugged with something. Yeah it happens and it was happening to me, GHB it's called, the date rape drug. Horse tranquilizer that Vets have on hand or sadly you can buy online without a Vet license if you are clever. Well... being the good ex-addict that I was with a hell of a high tolerance level built up over many bad years, it didn't hit me as hard as this guy had hoped. I tried to get up and leave, the bastard thought he was slick and tried to coerce me to go into his bedroom and lie on the bed till I felt better and he would just watch over me being the gentleman that he was. I got so damn mad at this asinine SOB. I mean seriously, we're '50 somethings' and you need a date rape drug to have sex with a woman! How freaking pathetic is that!

I staggered from the sunroom overlooking the ocean through the villa to the front room, I somehow got my few things fighting him off and ran and fell into my car and drove off. It had gotten dark quick and I was forty miles from home and driving down a winding stretch of A1A in a stupor. Using one hand to cover my left eye so I could keep the road somewhat in place, I focused on the yellow line and stayed as close to it as possible to avoid hitting anything along the roadside to my right until I got home... somehow. Only by the Lord's careful hand steering the car did I make that journey and I was made gracefully aware the Lord was indeed guiding me. Sadly or thankfully, the Lord had finally gotten my undivided attention about not only my weak judgment... but how little patience I had and how it would continue to betray me for far, into the future. Indeed, maybe it is a flaw in my character or simply a result of wanting badly to correct the sins of my past... right now! It would be many years and a few very lonely nights before I would try dating anyone. Luckily and thankfully for me, true blue Mark was always a phone call away as a trusted friend.

I like Mark a lot, this awesome friend was and is always there for me, including a night I was in serious distress. The meds I take cause serious gut problems if I don't eat right and for a time I was not following a very healthy diet. Mark was on his way to hang out with some of his cigar friends and was detoured by my call. I was in extreme pain and could barely talk when the phone stopped ringing and he picked up and I said; "Mark, please, I need your help, I can't drive myself and I need to go to the ER now!" Knowing exactly the amount of pain I lived with and the medications I took he had already witnessed a bad event I had a few months earlier.

"Ok, I will be there soon. I was just passing your street on my way out, give me 5 minutes." Thanking him I went and changed to be ready for my ride to the hospital hoping it would not be like the last time when I spent a week in the hospital getting me and my meds stabilized. I had been up for three straight days vomiting and I was now going into withdrawals from not being able to keep my medicine down. I was dehydrated and weak but Mark was able to get me to the hospital get me admitted and they immediately start running tests. The nurse spent fifteen minutes just trying to find a vein for the IV before going to find another nurse to give it a try. It took three more attempts before they were successful. It was a horrible night and the pain and convulsions damn near sent me into an irreversible shock. I survived it and there were a couple of pretty scary days but that's the cross I have to bear. It's one of the consequences of my addiction and the after-effects of organ malfunction for an extended period of time... over years. I've been there for Mark too. I saw him through his mother's death and other losses of security in his world. Good friends like Mark are hard to find as we rebuild our lives with a little trust, but I was finding that I needed to take these chances little by little. I never had this kind of just plain nonsexual male friends with the trust and closeness we share, but I do and I am grateful to the Lord I do.

Hospital visits aside, life was finally turning around three years on my own from Kurt and the security of having a steady mate and companion for good times and bad. But... I was making subtle little mistakes and overlooking things about myself I should not have been and still that sense of impatience was just nibbling away quietly at the security I had acquired in small steady steps. In my haste to move all things forward, I had not been praying or going to meetings for a few months, too busy with life and family. Something I had sworn I would not so easily forget again.

After work, one day Cat and I went down the street to our favorite little place by the water called The Drift House for some fresh air and ice tea. We found my favorite spot and sat down to watch the water roll in against the seawall and the little fishes below or the seagulls just above us waiting for a piece of bread to be thrown. I was happy anywhere near the water and this was one of my favorite places.

Cat says to me, "Soon I'll be done with my community service work and I won't have to deal with the Court's restrictions or Goodwill, and I'm off the hook for going to those meetings."

I asked her, "Why don't you want to continue with our meetings or staying clean?" I reminded her how much better her life had become and that just last week she had said so too, but Cat shrugged her shoulders and said; "I know but one more time won't hurt anything." I warned her every time I had used and relapsed that life got bad real fast. We were just starting right back up where we had left it and it always got progressively worse from there at a high rate of speed. Like a runaway freight train going 100 mph barreling down the tracks and the brakes had stopped working. Cat didn't seem to hear the knowledge I was trying to convey. All I could give her was the message and it would be up to her to follow its importance.

We had talked about how glad we were to have each other to talk to when things got crazy inside and recently I saw things were going that way for her, I had prayed for weeks that she would realize how using again would not end up good in any way shape or form. She began talking a few days later a whole lot about relapsing and I was worried. I had grown as much as I had because

I trusted my recovery sponsors and their advice and it kept me straight, I didn't want to lose my new friend to that life again. How could I make her understand she was heading for destruction? This is the same question asked daily by most everyone caring for someone in recovery. Knowing I couldn't go down that road ever again because it scared me to death to even think about it, I wanted to instill that fear in her but I could see that old glint in her eye that I had seen in mine many times before. I guess that perception was a gift and I truly wanted to apply it to her now and stop the train she was boarding.

I asked her, "Cat please tell me, what really did cause you so much pain? Sounds like you had a great life!" Up till now, Cathy had not talked much about her past and I believed she needed to talk about it now that maybe it would help if she did. They say in the rooms, the initial impact of 'getting it out' ultimately wells up so much pain from deep in your soul that it can be more... a lot more than some are ready to face.

Oh my God, the tears began to pour out as if a floodgate had just opened and Cathy cried for five minutes before stopping. I was horrified by what just happened and was so very sorry that I had even asked. Trying to calm her down I said, "Oh, I'm so sorry, I was just trying to help... please stop crying, it's going to be okay." Cat composed herself before revealing, "one evening I was leaving the mall in Boca Raton and I was grabbed, shoved into my car, and raped." It was the most brutal, ugly thing, I have ever dealt with and I guess using helps me escape from remembering it. The momentary terror of hearing her talk about her rape brought Pete racing through my mind. I could relate to her pain all too well. "Oh No, I'm so sorry Cathy" I shook my head to shake away those thoughts of Pete and the horror of any women being subjected to such violence.

"Damn, did they catch the bastard?" I asked.

She shook her head 'no' before she began to tell me the rest of what happened. "I was putting my bags into the backseat of my car, and I never saw him before he shoved me fully into the car, pulled up my dress, ripped off my panties, and raped me. I screamed Tiff and no one heard me, I was fighting him the best I could but he was too strong. The worst part was how long it lasted, it just went on and on like forever. It was late and the mall parking lot was nearly empty, so I guess I was an easy target, I should have been more aware, or something."

"No Cat, it was not your fault, don't ever think for one second it is or that you provoked his violence on you. Rape is a horrible thing I know, trust me." I said to her.

Being a product of long-term abuse, I had believed abuse to be a normal part of life, and never knowing a world of non-abuse, or that any other world existed beyond it, was the world I once lived in. But the hand of God ultimately pushed and pulled me into understanding there was a different world and He was guiding me there... one day at a time. I asked God to help my friend Cathy through her troubles and asked her to embrace a higher power and I reminded her of the strength it gave me on all those lost and scared nights now and in my past. I asked if she had ever gone to any domestic violence groups or victims of assault of any kind to help her with that pain. She said she had not. I encouraged her to do so and that getting the pain out through therapy was the only thing that helped me and I truly believe it could help her too.

"I know it's hard but you can recover from it, with daily dedication, you can change your life. Rape is such a terrible thing, truly ugly, forced, mean, and brutal. A painfully emotional trauma that is even more hurtful than the actual physical assault. All the violation of it is truly evil. The haunting reality of the assault in such a way never leaves you, though you can move on from it, with help. Seek some professional guidance or join a group to share with others who also have suffered this abuse," I calmly told her.

"What happened to you?

I know it's something, I can tell by the way you're looking at me," she asked.

Closing my eyes I say, "I was raped and it was horrible. It is almost impossible to move beyond but with help, I was able to and life is much better now."

"When?" she asked. "Well, unfortunately, more than once," I told her.

Cat just stared at me her eyes got as big as a saucer unable to speak just staring with a pained look in her eyes."When finally I shared it with my therapist it actually helped me for many reasons and now I see why, so I could share this hope with you. Being forced to have sex or perform any sexual thing is deplorable and terrible, things too horrible to speak of, the cruel acts of violence, are just too unreal for most people to even fathom," I explained to her.

Rape is Never Justified. With much therapy, I finally understood this fact and it allowed me to heal. Looking at Cathy I said to her, "Please get some help before it's too late and it eats you alive."

I was trying to build a trusting relationship with Cathy and I was worried about her. She would no longer have anyone except herself to hold her recovery in check and be responsible for her own recovery. For now, all I could really accomplish was getting Cat to see what relapsing was going to cost her. I wanted to start sharing my hope with others and God had put Cat there in my workplace to show me I could see those in need were everywhere. Unfortunately, I didn't see Cat at work again after that day. I didn't see her in the rooms we went to and I called but her phone was turned off. I felt so bad and sadly a few days later reading the newspaper I came across a story of a young woman, Cathy Smith from Boca Raton, Florida ... that had been found dead. I cried in deep anguish as I read the story. Cathy's pain was more than she could take and more than she was willing to fight for and it began with that all self-deception she could have 'just one drink' and having one drink too many, Cat in her despair for relapsing went looking for the final escape and found it. Death... and a gravestone.

Sadly this caused me to withdraw even further from people and

I began wondering to myself if it was somehow my fault because I had gotten her to talk about her rape? Addiction looks for these exact moments to pull you back, and it was at my doorstep. Was Cat gone because of her own fear to face the past? I wondered if anything could have been done to stop this tragedy from happening. Dealing with her death was difficult and I called my sponsor who told me something very important. She said, "Tiff just as no one could help you until you were ready to help yourself, the same is true for your friend." This is the worst and most difficult part of recovery. Acknowledgment of what has been and walking through those fears to what will be is scary and it is painful, but trusting you will get through it and to another day is important. I put away the self-blame and accepted I had done what I thought was right and I believed it was, but simply too little too late to change... Cat's choice.

I spent a few weeks thinking about Cat and thought it might be a good idea to change my own scenery and maybe some new friends in a new neighborhood. I moved into a 2-bedroom apartment setting up the second bedroom as my office to focus on working from home. My chronic pain condition was growing worse and being on my feet all day at the thrift store really was beyond my limits when added to the other body issues. I spent a few weeks applying for work hoping I could apply new knowledge and the growing amount of new perceptions about how the world really worked after ten years hiding away from the world.

I found a job I thought I might be good at. A large worldwide moving and storage company needed a trainee with a good attitude and good with people. Yep, that was me. Responsible for helping people each day placing reservations for their move, it was hard work and tremendously fast-paced. I had to learn quickly and be lightning-fast on the computer to make it all come together without too many, no not really, no mistakes at all. I couldn't send their stuff where they weren't going to ever be. Well... I got good at it, real quick. My new career was really good in a big way... when I got it correct, I felt a lot of self-esteem from all the good things

I got right from customers and a lot of praise from my bosses also for doing a great job almost from day one... or maybe it was two! I realized I likely had a very secure future too. I had the chance to build my retirement which at my age could be a really nice retirement if I stayed the course all the way through. Well in 2020 and Covid19 that reality would come to an end, as lives around the world came to first a screeching halt, as time moved at a snail's pace, and other ambitions were put on hold.

It was at this job and the voices on those phones, social media, and my own family, the Lord showed me there was pain and suffering everywhere. He knows well I had no earthly idea about that reality when I signed up. I was changed by talking to hundreds of people weekly and hearing the pain or anger from young girls who choose to flee from their abuser and needed help and encouragement to follow through with their plan, as well as helping them coordinate that escape. God had given me a new perception and by feeling their pain and hearing the fear in their voices, I always found a way to offer assurance offering words of hope and inspiration. I gave them positive words, it will get better by trusting their instincts for self-preservation their life could only improve from here and the struggles ahead and the new foundation they were making could be the happiness they wanted. The response with tears in their voices made me cry on many occasions, but I was sure I was making a difference. It was a win-win. I was building a sense of awareness and finding ways to help people in difficult moments, and they were helping me grow a better understanding of the world we were living in today. The Lord knows my destiny and I think he has steadily opened my eyes as a whole person, an individual making life choices I am accountable for, and consequences I will accept as they are.

12

My Sanctuary

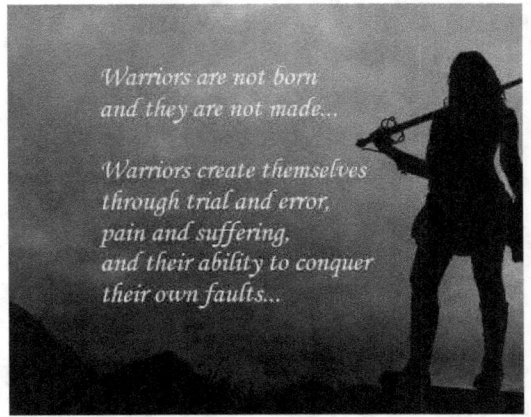

MY ADDICTION JOURNEY is not unique. Many others who became addicted have a similar story to tell and share in hopes we are all made better as we talk the talk and walk the walk of recovery together. Each of us adds something valuable to the collective journey that is ours when we offer up advice to a fellow traveler to assist them or speak to one and many at a meeting about insights we have found. We each and everyone took the first step into the experience of dependence the same way when we used that very first time, but from there on the road map, we followed far into confusion crossed many streets and avenues, drives and lanes, ways and courts, to arrive at the building called compulsion, our destination in the circle called addiction. There are a handful of universal experiences that we have each known walking casually down the stairs with a smile and little awareness it's a trap we are descending into until the lights suddenly go out and the lighted exit signs we ignored go off and the handrail that we didn't need going down isn't there to guide us up or down. In the darkness, we are immersed in confusion and dismay knowing yes we are addicted. The first panic of withdrawal ignites our fears we weaken we shudder we struggle with the choice we must make knowing we are stranded here in the gloom of cravings... but not helpless. Do we stay here in the dark or do we listen for a voice of hope to guide us out of the dungeon of our sickness and be rescued by a Warrior into our freedom.

Most all of us found our way into addiction through common mistakes in judgments and arrived at a dismal place called dependency and misery before we made the choice to be sober and determine which passage through recovery we would follow to freedom. A friend or family member, a spouse or a boss, a doctor or police officer, or maybe a Judge helped us make our choice to get sober and start and finish our recovery. My own choices and decisions about giving up my addiction began with high hopes and false starts called relapse and further destruction before I traveled the right passages leading me to permanent freedom. Someone or my Higher Power or maybe both heard my cries for help, turned on the lights, and I followed the nearest exit sign, and out I went into jail where my final recovery journey began.

When we hear and believe the voices of reason beckoning us to surrender our failed way of life, and listen and be guided by perceptive truths of those who learned their way out of addiction, we begin a marathon of choices and decisions to the finish line through the smoky rooms of recovery. Those who have gone and come back from the hell of addiction and made the right choices can be our best guides, and if they choose to offer or share their experience and knowledge of how it was done, are good souls of great compassion. There are also the countless individuals and organizations of people who mend our injuries and heal our pains that are saints on earth and worthy of praise. I chose to share with you some of the things I observed and learned from those saints and now pass them along to you in the best way I know-how. Hopefully, you will find some helpful insights and maybe a little humor as well, to make your journey through recovery more of an adventure than a hardship.

I rebuilt my life and found all that life held for me only by trusting God first in all things. Believing I will not fail myself again if I maintain a high level of awareness of what surrounds me and what I surround myself with, I have established limits and boundaries beyond which I must not and do not go. After God, my priorities are my health, my family, my career, and my friends in that order. I manage my life just as I did when I began my recovery journey, namely by a goal-oriented disciplined approach to structuring my time and my efforts to meet objectives established by needs and wants that are pretty much universal for most of us living in the good old USA. I work and I play, I rest and I sleep. Those four domains fill twenty-four hours of each day. As the verses from the Bible that found their way into a popular mainstream song in the 1960s made popular by a rock group called 'The Byrds' laments, "To everything, there is a time and a season." I remember during the time when I was in jail being guided by Sister Ann, Sister Doris offering me a book that was in her possession about mental discipline and its many benefits. I read it and reread it many times during the first two years of my freedom. It became the foundational instructions for planning and controlling my life and those practices or habits only got stronger and proved more beneficial right through today.

The very simple and easy-to-manage objectives set for a day, a week, a month, ad infinite for a lifetime fall into one of those four domains for me. I wrote down the objectives I had maintaining my recovery and sobriety such that if it's on my written list it happens and what isn't on the lists generally doesn't happen. I write down the things I need to do, want to do, and the goals that I want to achieve as far in advance as they need to be to know pretty much all the little steps and attributes I need to fill in a satisfactory plan for the rest of the life/time I expect to have on this earth... a little each day. Sunday is my first day of the week, I go to Church Sunday morning and I maintain my relationship with my boss the Lord and my Spirituality. I enjoy the good things I can in my leisure time after I have successfully completed the priorities of Sunday morning such as prepare the grill for an afternoon grilling hamburgers to share with family, friends, and neighbors who come over to my house to watch a football game. Sunday through Saturday the necessary everyday responsibilities of life are checked off the list.

Living life according to my planning and having time for everything has given me great fulfillment and has filled my life to capacity with the things I most cherish. I never over-plan but I never leave too much time that is unproductive. Just as I wanted to own my own home I achieved it by putting the goal in writing and working out the details steadily that finally made it possible. The joy of that long-term goal happened on the day of my twelfth year of sobriety. Wow! It is truly symbolic and it was the culmination of a well-planned well-executed achievement. I was extremely happy to pack up one last time and move from my little apartment and be a new independent homeowner. On Sept. 12, 2014, I rented a U-Haul truck and spent the next 24 hours slowly moving into my new home. This was what hard work and dedication to achieving a goal were all about and new lists were to be made as I enjoy this new sanctuary.

I had planned the work and worked the plan for twelve years, kind of symbolic like the Twelve Step program! If I had not planned it, as a reasonable objective I wanted to achieve in the early years of my recovery plan, I would have allowed numerous job denials and other life setbacks to deprive me of eventual success. It became clear to me as I achieved small short-term goals, it was important to learn how to navigate the short-term struggles to achieve long-term results. Throughout my journey, as I helped myself and helped others, I saw the importance and the powerful benefits of positive thinking to overcome multiple short-term defeats as ultimately resulting in long-term success. It will be what you believe it will be if you are willing to put in the work, exercise patience, and be a little flexible in your planning.

As I began planning what and how to help others, I needed to be honest with myself about the 'Why' that I was doing it.

Was the why – for money and fame, – NO!

I wrote about my life to invoke a warning to those who have not been devastated by the consequences of addiction, or believe that being a functional addict will never give them those life-ending results they never saw coming. As someone recently pointed out in a review of The Big Trap, "If you want to know what Addiction is just read this book."

I hope through the series I have brought together as I bore my life's story looking to reach others and help them avoid the trap, that they can embrace a new outlook in conquering the stigma of addiction & recovery as they rebuild body, mind, and soul. I wish everyone suffering from the battle of addiction, as well as the challenges of recovery much success in your new life, may it be filled with all you ever believed possible.

Let the Lord guide your journey to success always.
ROSE

www.ingramcontent.com/pod-product-compliance
Lightning Source LLC
Chambersburg PA
CBHW071156070526
44584CB00019B/2816